A HERCULE POIROT WHODUNNIT PUZZLE COLLECTION

The publishers would like to thank the following sources for their kind permission to reproduce the pictures in this book:

Dover Publications: 43, 166

iStockphoto: 24, 30, 41, 50, 52, 56L, 58T, 59TL, 65, 67, 152, 156, 164, 171, 175L, 177, 182

Mary Evans Picture Library: 14L, 14C, 17, 21, 26, 27, 29L, 36T, 36B, 39, 40, 44, 49, 57, 61, 62, 63, 69, 76, 77, 79BR, 81R, 84, 89, 93, 98, 103, 104, 107, 108, 113, 119, 121, 123, 138, 145L, 145C, 147, 150, 154, 155L, 160T, 160B, 162, 163, 167, 170, 176, 179, 180, 188, 189BR, 190R, 194, 196, 200, 204, 206, 207, 210, 222; /Alinari Archives: 136, 221; /Antiquarian Images: 135, 220; /H Armstrong Roberts/Classicstock: 114; /David Cohen Fine Art: 25, 153; /The David Pearson Collection: 16, 100, 101, 116, 146, 201, 202; /Dryden Collection: 54, 174; /Everett Collection: 11, 42, 165; /Francis Frith: 105, 205; /Grenville Collins Postcard Collection: 81L, 190L; /Illustrated London News: 23, 38, 47, 71, 95, 109, 151, 161, 168, 184, 198; /Imagno: 106; /Interfoto/TV-Yesterday: 94, 197; /Interfoto Agentur: 92, 124L, 215L; /Kevin Walsh Nostalgia Collection: 75, 187; /Maurice Collins Images Collection: 15, 87, 193; /Medici: 51, 96, 172, 199; /Metropolitan Police Authority: 18, 122; /Natural History Museum: 31, 48, 73, 128, 157, 169, 186, 217; /H L Oakley: 64, 181; /Onslow Auctions Limited: 131, 132, 143, 218, 219; /Petit Palais/Roger-Viollet/Irene Andreani: 12, 144; /Photo Researchers: 53, 173; /The Russell Butcher Collection: 13; /SZ Photo/Scherl: 68, 183; /Joanna Sanderson: 28, 79T; /Gill Stoker: 22; /TAH Collection: 14R, 145R; /Vanessa Wagstaff Collection: 124C, 124R, 215C, 215R

Shutterstock: 19, 20, 29R, 32, 33, 37, 45L, 56R, 72, 74, 78, 79BL, 80, 82, 85, 86, 88, 90, 97L, 97R, 99, 102L, 110, 111, 112, 115, 117, 118, 125, 126, 129, 134, 139, 140, 148, 149, 155R, 158, 175R, 185, 189BL, 192, 203L, 208, 209, 211, 212, 213, 216, 223

Every effort has been made to acknowledge correctly and contact the source and/or copyright holder of each picture, and Carlton Books Limited apologises for any unintentional errors or omissions, which will be, corrected in future editions of this book.

This is a Carlton Book
Published in 2016 by Carlton Books Limited
20 Mortimer Street, London W1T 3JW

ISBN 978-1-78097-828-4

10 9 8 7 6 5 4 3 2
Printed in China

A HERCULE POIROT WHODUNNIT PUZZLE COLLECTION

EXERCISE YOUR LITTLE GREY CELLS
TO SOLVE OVER 100 RIDDLES,
CONUNDRUMS AND CRIMES INSPIRED BY
AGATHA CHRISTIE'S GREAT DETECTIVE

TIM DEDOPULOS

CARLTON
BOOKS

"IF YOU ARE TO BE HERCULE POIROT, YOU MUST THINK OF EVERYTHING."

Agatha Christie

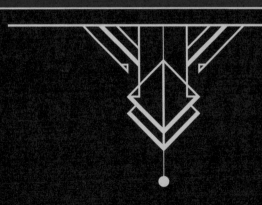

5

CONTENTS

PUZZLES## PUZZLES

Gentle Introductions ... 12

Charity ... 13

Three Children ... 14

Leases ... 15

Murderous Work ... 16

Policemen ... 17

Prison ... 18

Fighters ... 19

Miner ... 20

The Meeting ... 21

Inn's Mouth ... 22

Two Trains ... 24

Forgotten Places ... 25

Exercise ... 26

The Crowd ... 27

Matters of Life and Death ... 28

Guarded ... 29

Playing with Numbers ... 30

Portal ... 31

Children ... 32

A Sterner Test ... 33

The Suspicious Package ... 34

Husbandry ... 36

Cipher ... 37

Crate ... 38

The Wild Man ... 39

Social Lives ... 40

Watching Out ... 41

Gang ... 42

Mayfair ... 43

Brian ... 44

Intuition ... 45

Track ... 46

Dubious Proposition ... 48

Voyage, Voyage ... 49

Sideways ... 50

The Display ... 51

Carstairs ... 52

Global ... 53

The Bicycle ... 54

Deduction................................55

The Thin Black Line......................56

Societal................................57

Replication..............................58

Liars, Liars.............................60

Father..................................61

The Wheel...............................62

Black Hat...............................63

The Miracles of Birth....................64

A Simple Matter.........................65

A Second Deduction......................66

Eccentricities...........................67

Carolingians............................68

The Cart................................69

The Cost of Living.......................70

Luggage................................72

Fruit...................................73

A Simple Little List......................74

Stafford................................75

The Hospital............................76

Essential Knowledge.....................77

Dogmatic...............................78

Mental Juggling.........................80

French Goods...........................81

Another Cipher..........................82

Ritual..................................83

Blessings...............................84

Ancestry...............................85

A Trial.................................86

Fine Ale................................87

The Killer..............................88

Pigs...................................89

Sticky.................................90

Working up High........................91

Cliff..................................92

A Leisurely Voyage......................94

Eastbourne.............................95

Facts.................................96

Truth.................................97

Cat and Mouse.........................98

Drury Lane.............................99

Lumbering............................100

Monk.................................101

Courtyard.............................102

Miscreants 103

The Countryside 104

Upstanding 105

The Duchess of Ashford 106

Musical Chairs 108

Athletic 109

Outerwear 110

Vipers 111

Infernal Devices 112

Fowl 113

Smear 114

The Lamp 115

Sensitive Topics 116

Probable Causality 117

Fair Warning 118

Safe 119

The Channel 120

Self-evident 122

Barton 123

Triad 124

Ales 125

The Fire 126

Carolling 127

Three Doors 128

Children 129

Cross Rail 130

Luncheon 132

Invoicing 133

Deceptions 134

Orrery 135

The Explorer 136

Crowds 137

Hound 138

The Farm 139

Justified 140

Curtain 141

ANSWERS 144

INTRODUCTION

I was born, my dear friends, in the town of Spa, in Belgium. The start of the new century has not been gentle to my hometown, yet it retains a certain nobility and charm. This is undoubtedly aided by the abundant mineral springs, which, as well as producing a steady channel of wealth, also have led to its name being copied the world over.

Perhaps there is a hint of truth that the springs can offer benefits of health. *Certainement*, I myself partook frequently of the waters as a youth, at the urgings of my poor mother. Did this heighten the prodigious powers of my little grey cells? Who can say? At the very least, the waters, they did no harm.

I joined the police force of the magnificent city of *Bruxelles* in the last decade of the nineteenth century. From there, my progress was as rapid as, I am certain *mes amis*, that you keenly have anticipated. When the Great War broke out, I was forced to leave my position as the Chief of Police for Brussels, and flee to England. There, I found to my delight a warm welcome, and a new home. I rekindled my acquaintance with my dear friend Hastings, and was soon sought by the British government in matters of exquisite sensitivity.

From there... ah, but you will know of my adventures, *n'est-ce pas*? Let us say just that I have dedicated myself with singular attention to the downfall of the murderer and malefactor, wherever he or she is to be found. The most vital tool in this quest has been the mind – my own and my quarry's, both. It is of the most critical importance to have a perfect idea of the psychology of the murderer, the arrogance that leads him to the certainty that another's life is his to quench.

The mind, my dear friends, is a thing of patterns. The killer must fit the crime. By understanding the little grey cells, you can strive for perfection in yourself and for transparency in others. Then, there is nothing more to do than to encourage your foe, and those around him, to talk. In speech, the truths and lies will separate, become clear, show you facts and deceptions. When you have sufficient facts, you will always discover that they can fit together in only one way. Always. If there is lack of clarity, there is lack of fact.

I suggest to you most strongly that while you peruse this volume, you are to keep a stern awareness for that which is factual. The little grey cells, they respond well to stimulation. This is therefore my gift to you, a little *je ne sais pas* to help you exercise that which matters most. Enjoy, *mes amis*. Enjoy.

— HP, Whitehaven Mansions, London.

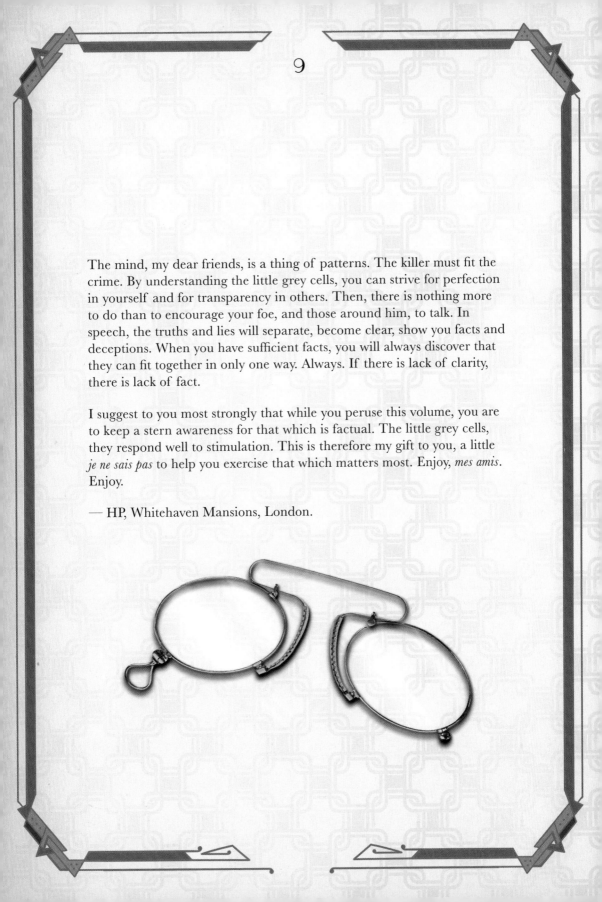

"IT IS THE BRAIN, THE LITTLE
GREY CELLS ON WHICH ONE
MUST RELY. ONE MUST SEEK THE
TRUTH WITHIN - NOT WITHOUT."

Hercule Poirot

PUZZLES

Gentle Introductions

MES AMIS, I THINK THAT I SHOULD BEGIN WITH YOU GENTLY.
The little grey cells, they need time to warm up, no? It is for the best. We all require a little help to become started so I shall address to you a rather simple matter.

I assume that you are sitting comfortably. Some of you may be lying down instead, having taken to your beds, but that is no matter. I would like you, at least in your imaginings, to sit a little less comfortably. The position I have in mind is one of sitting straight in a rather plain chair of the sort found at dinner tables. A straight back, a firm and flat seat, and so on. And you are in it, with your shins vertical, your thighs horizontal, and your back vertical again.

In this position, attempt to get up without allowing yourself to indulge in either leaning forward or bringing your feet backward. Try it! You will find it is quite impossible.

Why is this?

CHARITY

IT WAS THE SISTER OF CHARITY WHITE WHO FOUND HER, STRUCK DOWN MOST HORRIBLY in the very process of making herself a cup of tea. With the kettle still whistling insistently, Vera was scared to even cross to Charity's side, in case the assailant was still in the house.

The police failed to make any significant progress on the case for several days, at which point Vera sought my assistance. Her suspicions fell squarely on Charity's husband, Reed. Although her distaste for the man undoubtedly coloured her suspicions, Reed White was not the sort of fellow to inspire trust. He had a history of foul temper, and exhibited more paranoia and ill humour than grief regarding his wife's loss.

The police, of course, had already ruled out Reed as a suspect. He had arrived at a local pub an hour before Vera's discovery, and been there the entire time. The kettle could not have possibly been boiling for even half as long. His alibi was quite sound. Thus, I decided to focus my investigation on him. You see why, I trust?

ANSWER ON PAGE
144

ᎢHREE CHILDREN

FOR THE CLEAR MIND, IT IS ALWAYS NECESSARY TO DEAL WITH WHAT IS KNOWN FOR SURE, and not with what is assumed, or presumed, or otherwise arrived at without regard for absolute fact. This is simple, yes? I hope it is so, my friends. Unlike certain other so-called detectives, Hercule Poirot does not engage in flights of fancy, or imagine that a splash of mud is some unique clue.

In this situation, we have three children of a proud parent. This is how it should be, surely? Ah, parental pride, such a warming emotion! No child should have to do without. For this trio, at one time, the ages of two of the children, added together, was equal to that of the third. We shall call this "occasion one". Some further time later, yes, "occasion two" – two of the ages totalled double that of the remaining child. "Occasion three" is when the number of years since occasion one is two-thirds of the three children's combined ages on that occasion one.

For the period of several months that occasion three is true, one of the trio is aged 28. How old are the other two for that time?

ANSWER ON PAGE
145

QEASES

THE HOME IS THE CASTLE, THE ENGLISH SAY. HERCULE POIROT FEELS THAT THERE IS a quite obvious difference between the two. At least, that is so for most people. Still, who am I to deny the English their *charmante* little *excentrictés*? For such a nation, where a home is such a fortification against the invasions of neighbours and other armies, the practice of purchasing a lease on a property seems… whimsical.

Still… I met a fellow recently who owned a leasehold property, a fairly typical term of 99 years. To me, that seems another *excentricté*. The missing year, she is some magical sacrifice? It matters not. After a short discussion, I ascertained that four-fifths of the years remaining on the lease equalled two-thirds of the years already lapsed. Surely you can now tell me how many years remain, yes?

MURDEROUS WORK

A VERY NASTY AFFAIR THIS WAS, MES AMIS – VERY NASTY INDEED! A popular accountant was found dead in his office. He was found with his throat cut, slumped onto his desk, when his poor secretary arrived for work. The police informed me that when they moved the man, they found that the cut was clean, probably done with a razor. There was nothing legible remaining of his documents, which were soaked in blood. I trust that the dangers of coming to work in the early morning are clear: when you are the only person there, you have no potential witnesses to protect you from killers.

The partners were shocked, of course. Neither could give any reason why their colleague would have been so brutally murdered. The elder said that the victim had seemed stressed, and there were rumours of… indelicacies, but he himself had no trouble with the deceased. The younger was cooler, and hinted that perhaps the death was not for himself a disaster, but knew of no business or play that would motivate such action. The secretary could add only that the dead man had been working on the finances of a perfectly regular and boring company when attacked, and knew of no other client whose affairs might stray to the violently criminal.

The identity of the likely killer was immediately obvious, *naturallement*. I trust you have picked out the culprit?

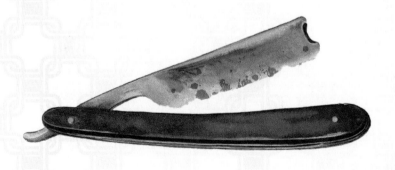

ANSWER ON PAGE
146

ꝐOLICEMEN

I NOTED RECENTLY THAT INSPECTOR JAPP SEEMED EVEN LESS LIVELY AND INTELLECTUALLY engaged than was usually the case. Dear Hastings seemed a little startled at such a pronouncement, but he did have to reluctantly agree. It was revealed then that the winter flu had cut a broad swathe through the ranks of Japp's detectives, and the few that remained hale were being forced to work most uncongenial hours.

How *terrible*!

The good Inspector seemed a little vague on the whole matter, but I was able to ascertain that Japp himself had now worked more nights in a row than his deputy, a man named Southwell, who had managed only four. An unfortunate fellow by the name of Collins had now worked 15 nights without break, more than Japp and Southwell combined. Ward had worked for nine nights, less than Japp.

How many nights had the resolute Japp now worked?

ANSWER ON PAGE
147

PRISON

THERE ARE MANY TYPES OF PRISON, MY FRIENDS. SOME ARE SOLID, and range from the horribly medieval to the gilded little cage. Others are of the emotion, imposed by guilt or envy, or fear or their kinds. Still more are from the mind, rigid walls of teacherly indoctrination and social acceptability. All of these prisons are bad. Beware convictions, I tell you. They will transform you, *là*, into a convict! In a certain prison, one that is the most accurately described as an idea, there is a lock with six dials. The first dial bears the letters A–Z, and then the remaining five each hold the numbers 0–9. Correctly guessing the total number of possible combinations of the dials will spring the lock open. What do you think?

ƑIGHTERS

I HAVE ALWAYS RATHER LIKED FIGHTER PILOTS: THEY ARE
HIGHLY OBSERVANT AND ADEPT, with the confidence that comes from
being a master of a rare and valuable skill. This is balanced by the humility of
the understanding that any ace can fall, and sooner or later, will do so. Warfare is
a matter of luck as well as skill, and any pilot who survived the Great War knows
full well that it could have been very different.   Hastings and I found ourselves
in the RAF Club, talking to a group of pilots last week, and they were very
hospitable and entertaining. It transpired that Wing Commander Loeb flew a
Fairey Firefly, Wing Commander Hannah a Bristol Jupiter and Flight Lieutenant
Mainwaring a Hawker Danecock. From this, do you suppose that Squadron
Leader Romanoff flew a Westland Interceptor, a Gloster Nightjar, a Vickers
Vireo, or a De Havilland Dormouse?

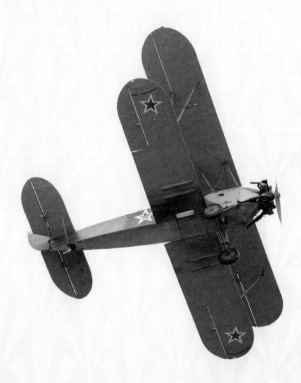

ANSWER ON PAGE
148

ᴍINER

A MAN I KNEW A LITTLE BIT, A FRIEND OF A FRIEND, CAME
TO ME LAST SUMMER to seek my advice. He had been speaking with an
Australian prospector, who was in London seeking investment to start working
a seam of gold. This seam he had discovered on a piece of land he'd obtained
the rights to recently, and he had quickly realized that effective extraction was
way beyond his prior operation. The terms he offered were generous, but not
startlingly so, and it was not unknown for Australians to seek British financial
support. I agreed to meet the man, and give an opinion on his reliability.

The prospector was in his early fifties, a tall, muscular man with weathered
hair and skin. His clothes were of reasonable quality, and he seemed fairly
cosmopolitan in conversation. I asked him about the site, and he was happy to
provide details, if not location.

"My claim is in the hills of Cape York, in the north. It's hot, sweaty country. A
river runs through the site, out of the mountains, heading east to the sea, and I've
cleared space for a simple hut on the right-hand bank. There's more shade there,
on the north side. The local vegetation is a nightmare, though. The gold's in a
long, low granite cliff, marbling the stone, but the entire area is overgrown with
trees, vines, spiders, all kinds of nonsense. Just getting the cliff face cleared out
for decent access would take me a year, on my own. I can't trust any of the local
lads. I need to get some boys in from Port Douglas or Brisbane, get on this sharp.
That's why I'm here."

I'm sure you understand why I felt confident in telling my acquaintance to have
nothing to do with the man, yes?

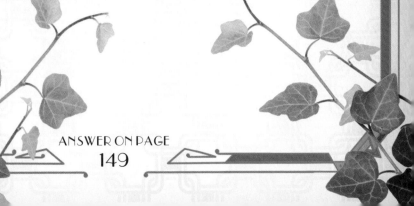

ANSWER ON PAGE
149

THE MEETING

DO YOU KNOW WHAT THE MORNING REQUIRES, *MES AMIS*?
It is simple! It requires a sharp knife to open the mail, enough space to sort that mail into the four piles, and a large mug of hot chocolate. Do you know what the morning does *not* require?

Meetings.

Nevertheless, sometimes meetings must happen. But this unhappy circumstance does offer me a small tutelary opportunity. Let us suppose that you are part of a circle of 12 people. Perhaps you are a committee of some sort, you poor souls! It is decided – how, it matters not – that seven of your number must assemble early in the morning tomorrow, to discuss items of interminable tedium.

From this stricture, how many different groups of seven could be assembled from your 12? More importantly, if the members are selected randomly, what is the chance that you would be permitted a lie-in?

ꟼNN'S ᴍOUTH

I RECALL MY DEAR HASTINGS CONVEYING THE PAIR OF US TO A TRADITIONAL PUB of some repute, in order to sample their culinary delights, such as they were purported to be. I did not hold out much of the hope, you understand. Britain is wonderful in a great many ways, but her cuisine is not equal to that of Belgium, or even of France. I am confident that this is not a controversial statement. Who but the British would boil minced beef, I ask? Answer not, please. I fear my poor, ever-sensitive stomach would be most unhappy.

Still… To the inn I went. Standing inside the entrance, we were somewhat dismayed to discover the place to be utterly full of customers. Hastings made a noise of saddened dismay. To distract him from his disappointment, I suggested that we pretend each person was in possession of a different, but consecutive, number of shillings and further, that there were more guests than any single one of them had shillings. Hastings, in turn, nervously asked if next I would tell him to imagine them all naked. *Mon Dieu!* No, I assured him. Instead, if we posited that there was no person with 38 shillings on his or her person, then that would tell us the maximum number of guests possible.

Hastings pointed out that he could just count them, if he so cared. You, *mon ami*, have not that luxury. What was their number, assuming my suppositions to be accurate?

ANSWER ON PAGE
151

ꟼWO ꟼRAINS

FACTS ARE THE ENTIRETY OF DETECTIVE WORK. WITH ENOUGH FACTS, and a clear understanding of what is not reliable information but merely treacherous instinct or assumption, the true story of any situation must, of itself, unfold before you.

So imagine, if you please, two trains passing each other in the opposite direction. From the viewpoint of the driver of the slower train, the two trains are passing for five seconds. *Eh bien!* Now imagine the two trains again, this time passing each other in the same direction. The driver, he notes that this operation requires 15 seconds.

If I inform you – as I am now doing – that the faster train is 200 feet in length, and the slower train twice that, you will be able to tell me the speed of the faster train in feet per second. Yes?

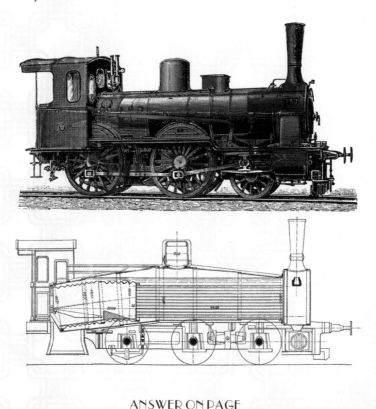

ANSWER ON PAGE
152

FORGOTTEN PLACES

I HAVE ALLUDED ELSEWHERE TO THE UNPLEASANTNESS OF MEDIEVAL DUNGEONS. Man is most inventive in his brutality. Ah, if only he was as diligent and creative in the spreading of joy and equity! Alas, my work as the bane of the criminal is not likely to end any time soon. But dungeons! The nastiest of these forgotten places had the form of a flaring hole in the earth, dug so that the circular walls angled inwards toward the hole at the top, far overhead. The unfortunate occupant was thrown inside, and left to fester. Such places were usually constructed underground, for reasons that should come easily to your mind.

One fortunate – or *unfortunate*, according to your situation – side effect of this placement was to make these *oubliettes* almost impossible to tunnel out of. One would have to make a tunnel big enough for oneself, long enough to reach not only the height of the *oubliette* but the full way to the surface, and avoid tunnelling into other constructions along the way.

But then, if one was digging, perhaps one would not have to tunnel at all in order to escape. Do you see my meaning?

EXERCISE

I ONCE HAD THE INESTIMABLE CAPTAIN HASTINGS FOLLOW A MAN AROUND LONDON FOR ME. It is the sort of thing that Hastings is eminently suited for. He is a strong believer in the importance of the action physical. Of course, he does not have to maintain his little grey cells in anything like the perfection that I must labour for. No, if one of us is to run around, it is he.

On his return, Hastings told me that the man, unaware of his secret companion, had caught a bus to an area south of the river. The man had alighted from the bus, dropped an item into a public bin, and then walked the precise bus route back to his point of origin. The whole process took six hours, with the bus averaging 12mph, and the walking a third of that speed.

I assured him that his observations were vitally useful, and he was as pleased as a puppy. Perhaps you will tell me how long the route was?

THE CROWD

LET US VENTURE INTO ANCIENT WISDOM FOR A MOMENT, MY FRIENDS. PICTURE, if you please, a lone fellow, a bishop, facing a modest crowd. Religion is a fine thing for those who need its comforts. Matters of the divine do not generally concern me, however. The hand of God, in my experience, is fitted entirely within the glove of the laws of nature, and it is that glove that matters to my work. But religion, for many centuries, kept the spark of knowledge alive, and our friend here is the exemplar of such feats. His words are peculiar, as befits a Yorkshireman of his far-away time, but illuminating nonetheless.

"Oh, that there are as many more of you are you are now, and then half of half of this number were added to you, and another half of this again added to your number, why, then with me, we would together number a full hundred."

How many men did the Bishop face?

ANSWER ON PAGE
154

MATTERS OF LIFE AND DEATH

AH, LIFE, SHE IS SO VERY FRAGILE! THERE ARE SO MANY WAYS BY WHICH IT MAY BE SNUFFED. Sometimes I wonder that any of us survive our initial years… yet we do. What a triumph of hope we truly are! Yes, even worthy Japp.

There were two men, both of whom are now dead. The first, he died in 1812 – an ominous year, for certain. The second, we know to have died 140 years after the birth of the first. Through my talents, I have discovered for sure that their combined lifespan totals 125 years.

Be of good cheer, my friends! With such knowledge as you now possess, can you now inform me of the year of birth of the second man?

CA 962796

CERTIFIED COPY of an ENTRY OF BIRTH.
Pursuant to the Births and Deaths Registration Acts, 1836 to 1929.

Registration District SUNDERLAND

GUARDED

MEN OF VIOLENT INTENT AND BEHAVIOUR ARE INCLINED TO EXPECT VIOLENCE where most other people would see only pleasant things, such as cake, or a glass of fine wine. It is a terrible prison they build for themselves, fearing always the retribution, which they know – from horrible experience – that can come at any time. For have they not dished the same out again and again?

I once met with a man so wicked, so terrified, that he kept a pair of guards with him at all times, whatever room he was in. It is said they even accompanied him to his toilet, which I do not wish to imagine. These guards were stoic to extremes that would make the guards of the King look flighty. Although the pair stood facing opposite directions, either side of the man, and always stared straight ahead, they still managed to closely observe both their charge and the whole room he occupied. Mirrors were not involved in this feat, nor other machines or technologies of any kind.

How do you think they did it?

ANSWER ON PAGE
155

PLAYING WITH NUMBERS

DO NOT BE AFRAID OF TURNING FROM THE CONCRETE REALITY TO THE ABSTRACT THOUGHT, *mes amis.* On the first of the hands, there is always the possibility that the seemingly intangible may eventually come to practical life around you. This happens more often than you think. The real world can turn into numbers at the drop of a pin. Then, on the second of the hands, there is the value of strengthening the mental muscles for their own sake. The little grey cells, they do not respond well to neglect, *non?* Ignore them, let them fester, and the body will channel their nutrients to other areas that you do use, such as your brawny legs, or your digestive tract. The little grey cells will starve. Alas, poor Hastings!

So, let us consider something of abstraction. There are four whole numbers I wish you to find. Each one is different. To one, add 2, and you will get x. For the second, multiply by 2, and you will get x. The third, you divide by 2 to get x. The fourth has 2 subtracted to, yes, again give you x. Added together, these four numbers will total 45.

What are they?

ANSWER ON PAGE
156

PORTAL

IS THERE EVER A STERNER TEST OF THE LITTLE GREY CELLS THAN THOSE OCCASIONS when there is something of great importance at stake? To remain calm and clear of thought when the emotions are riled, and the pressure is mounting, these are the moments that truly define the character.

So… Let us imagine that you find yourself at the end of a hallway, in front of a pair of doors. Behind one door is something strictly undesirable, such as a ravenous and extremely angry tiger, which, alas, you cannot hear or otherwise detect, due to the exquisite soundproofing of the doorway. The other door is less certain. Perhaps it holds a second tiger, but perhaps it holds something equally desirable. A wondrous *gâteau*, let us say.

There are two notes, which had formerly adorned the doors, but now lie on the floor. One says, "This door holds back a tiger". The other says, "Both doors hold back tigers". On the wall, a slightly longer missive explains that only if the sign on the first door is true, that door hides a cake. Likewise, if the sign on the second door is false, that door hides a cake. There certainly is a cake, it adds. Perhaps not here, but somewhere… And it is wonderful!

Which door should you open?

ANSWER ON PAGE
157

CHILDREN

PERHAPS YOU ARE DUE A SIMPLE LITTLE TRIFLE, MY FRIENDS. THE LITTLE GREY CELLS, they need a moment here and there in order to recharge, *n'est-ce pas?* It does not do to pile on the mental work without any end. All too soon, the brain becomes *fatigué*, and then the thoughts follow into sluggish dullness. This will never do!

So, and so… A mother, she has two children. If I inform you that one of them is a girl, then how likely is it that the other one is a boy? Does it make a difference if I inform you that the girl just mentioned was her *first* child? You may assume, for this case only, that there is an equal likelihood of any child being male or female.

ANSWER ON PAGE
158

A STERNER TEST

NOW THAT YOUR LITTLE GREY CELLS ARE ALL REFRESHED
AND RELAXED, LET US ATTEMPT A STERNER CHALLENGE.

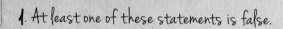

1. At least one of these statements is false.

2. At least two of these statements are false.

3. At least three of these statements are false.

4. At least four of these statements are false.

5. At least five of these statements are false.

6. At least six of these statements are false.

7. At least seven of these statements are false.

8. At least eight of these statements are false.

9. At least nine of these statements are false.

10. At least ten of these statements are false.

How many of these statements are true?

ANSWER ON PAGE
159

THE SUSPICIOUS PACKAGE

MY GOOD FRIENDS, AS YOU KNOW, I AM OFTEN CALLED UPON TO ASSIST SCOTLAND YARD with matters that are beyond their ingenuity. It is a stern duty, but one to which Hercule Poirot submits without complaint. No matter the inconvenience, I am always available for the police – to their considerable good fortune.

One afternoon, I was approached by Inspector Japp regarding a package, which had been shipped to a town in Hookland on a train that morning. Because of certain obfuscations in the processing and weighing of the train's cargo, the Inspector was unable to ascertain clearly which of the packages was the one he needed to observe. It is curious, the inefficiencies which are found in your United Kingdom.

The train had carried five packages, which I will label A to E for you. Documentation secured by the good Japp specified that packages D and E together weighed 10 pounds, B and C collectively weighed 12½ pounds, A and B 13 pounds, C and D 13½ pounds, and finally, that all three of A, C and E came to 18 pounds.

Which package was the heaviest?

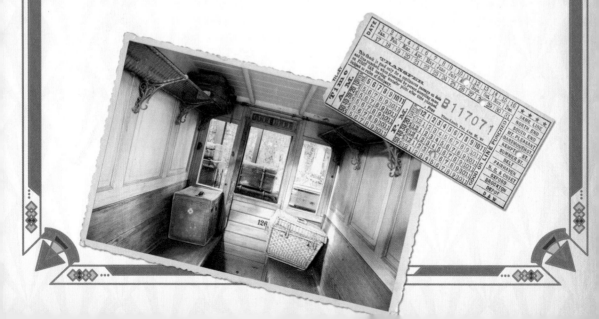

ANSWER ON PAGE
159

HUSBANDRY

I HAVE THE GREATEST ADMIRATION FOR FARMERS. FOR THEM, THE WEARYING DAILY challenge of brutal exertion, of the early start and the cruel weather, of cold and rain and scorching sun. For us, the tastiest of morsels! Is there any greater symptom of human development than the decoupling of personal labour from the personal feeding? Ah, how our earliest ancestors must have dreamed of such a thing!

Let us picture three cows of differing ages – and sizes – at home in a field of pasture. This may be a rather idyllic proposition, I recognize, but you may consider it a metaphor if that makes you feel easier. We shall call these cows A, B, and C, for who knows the true names of cows? Not Hercule Poirot, that is for certain.

Left to their own devices, A and B would consume the pasture entirely in 45 days. A and C would do the same in 60 days. B and C would manage such a thing in 90 days. But we have A, B and C – how long will the pasture survive, discounting possible regrowth?

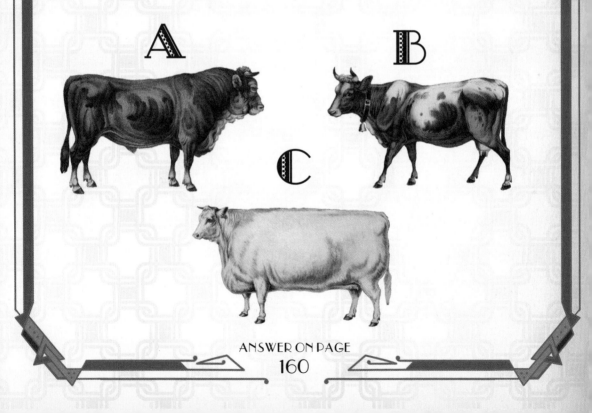

ANSWER ON PAGE
160

CIPHER

IT IS A SIMPLE YET REGRETTABLE TRUTH THAT MANY OF THOSE INVOLVED IN NEFARIOUS BUSINESS turn to codes and ciphers in order to coordinate their crimes with their fellow conspirators while still obscuring plans from prying observers. Fortunately for the detective, most criminals are of lazy intellect at best – for honestly, while crime does often pay, it is a dangerous business, and the hours required can be astonishingly long. There are much better ways of attaining wealth, if one is clever.

The result is that most ciphers used by criminals are quite straightforward, lacking in any real ingenuity. With a little practice in the art, it becomes quite possible to deal with them effectively.

Below are five districts of the broad Greater London area, each encrypted with the same cipher:

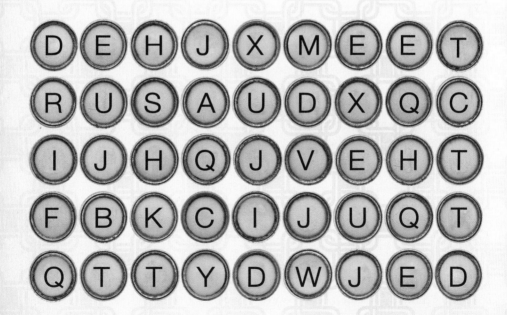

What are they?

ANSWER ON PAGE
161

CRATE

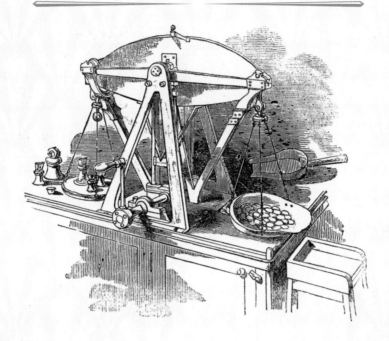

LET US MAKE USE OF OUR IMAGINATIONS ONCE AGAIN,
mes amis. There is, in front of us, a crate of metals, which, together, weigh a substantial 37½ pounds – that is, 600 ounces. It contains four different metals: gold, silver, brass and tin.

The proportions of the metals are in strict variance by weight. There is three times as much silver as there is gold, there is three times as much brass as there is silver, and there is three times as much tin as brass. The advantage here of the imagination, it must be very clear, *oui*? Quite apart from the discomfort of having to deal with almost 40 pounds by weight of assorted metals, obtaining such specimens would be both costly and inconvenient. Far better to use the labour of the mind than the labour of the pick!

So, how much gold is there in the crate, in ounces?

ANSWER ON PAGE
161

THE WILD MAN

I WAS ONCE CALLED TO HELP A BARRISTER WITH A MATTER REGARDING AN ASSAILANT who had attempted to despatch his mother to the next world most unpleasantly. This was late one persistently rainy night of the sort that you British seem to indulge in so regularly. Fortunately for the family, their maid was in the library, re-shelving a few books before bed, some two or so hours before the attack. She spied an unfamiliar man watching the house covertly from the nearby wood, and had the foresight to make some notes on his appearance – if not enough, alas, to call the police.

According to the witness, the man was unkempt of hair and clothing, but tall and strongly built. A distinctive break in his nose provided a vital hint to his identity. The barrister admitted to me that he had seen fit to sack a gardener some years before, for unspecified but perfidious activities. The man seen by the maid was strongly reminiscent of the gardener's surly son.

Naturallement, I was immediately convinced of the son's absolute innocence. You can see why?

ANSWER ON PAGE
162

SOCIAL LIVES

LET US MOVE ONCE MORE THE HISTORICAL TO THE HYPOTHETICAL. There is much to be learned by and through postulation. It is the essence of scientific enquiry, *non*? Without it, how are we to formulate our notions? *Eh bien*! I could continue, but it is enough to suppose that you accept hypothesis to be of great merit, and move on. If you do not, well, I would despair, except that you are not currently standing in front of me to inform me of the inaccuracy of my modest suppositions.

So, you and your partner are attending a dinner party with four other long-standing couples. Perhaps you are even hosting it. I am certain that the food and wine will be impeccable. You would stand for nothing less, I feel sure. Again, I feel safe in this presumption. Looking at your guest list, to your amazement you realize that none of the other nine party-goers have previously met the same number of attendees. That is, the other nine have, between them, previously met one to nine of the rest of the attendees. You are of course counting yourself among this category of "the rest of the attendees".

Clearly, one must be familiar with one's own partner, and if A has met B, then B has met A. So how many of the attendees have you yourself previously met?

ANSWER ON PAGE
163

WATCHING OUT

I AM HIGHLY AVERSE TO MY TIME AND EXPERTISE BEING PAID FOR ON A BASIS of elapsed time. Such things are notoriously slippery, and can easily lead to treacheries of the most mundane sort. It is a lesson I learned early on in my career, and now I am most careful to bill by result, not by the hours used in attaining it.

I engaged to assist a fellow with a string of robberies at his warehouse that had recently turned violent. We agreed that I would give him 30 days of my time in return for £100. I say this not to boast, merely to provide information that you will require.

In the event, I solved the matter in 18 days, and to my surprise, received just £10 and a wristwatch that my client insisted was quite valuable. This, he maintained, fairly recompensed me for time used. I did not agree, but that is by the by. If we generously pretend that he was playing fairly, what would be the worth of the watch?

ANSWER ON PAGE
164

GANG

I ONCE LED THE POLICE TO A GROUP OF UNPLEASANT BRAVOS WHO HAD perpetrated a string of unusually violent robberies along the South Coast. Such things are all too common. I remember this pack because they were all from good, if modest, backgrounds. It is sad how the world will sometimes lead previously decent people into horrible actions.

From my memory, I will share with you some information about the gang members' names, roles, former jobs and distinguishing features. The man with facial scarring was the gang's driver, but was not either Richard or Jimmy. The gang's thug, who specialized in intimidation, had previously been a potter. The gang's locksmith had been a farmer; this was not Derek, who had a bad knee, and could not kneel. Gordon, who had tattooed knuckles, had not formerly been a farmer. The man with the flat nose was not the gang's con man. Richard was a former porter, and had a knife wound in his arm. Neither Brian nor Gordon was the former teacher. One of the men had been a miner. Lastly, one of the men was the gang's strategic planner.

So, what role was performed by the man with a knife wound in his arm?

MAYFAIR

I HAD THE GREAT FORTUNE, EXACTLY THREE YEARS AGO IN MAYFAIR, of meeting the Misses Thompson, Adele and Beatrice. The former is the aunt of the latter, but their relationship is closer to that of mother and daughter. Alas, the parents of the lovely Beatrice perished in a boating accident when she was but young!

Upon introduction, I naturally exclaimed, *en charmant*, that surely I was meeting a pair of sisters. This produced the amusement I had desired. I was justly rewarded when Beatrice informed me that in fact the pair were the same age – if you swapped the order of the digits of one of their ages, that is. Without such manipulation, 45 years stood between the pair.

I smiled, and explained how difficult I found that sum to believe. Adele patted my arm gratefully, and confided that added together, the digits of her age produced a square number. Instantly, their true ages were revealed to me, but I was not so crass as to allude to that fact.

How old is Beatrice today?

ANSWER ON PAGE
166

BRIAN

I KNOW A YOUNG MAN OF STERN CHARACTER NAMED BRIAN.
Hastings finds him quite impossible, but I have no such qualms. What my dear friend mistakes for a dour lack of humour is in fact a wit so sharp and dry that it reminds me of desert creatures. It infuriates poor Hastings when I erupt into laughter in the midst of a seemingly deadly serious conversation with Brian, with the latter paying my amusement apparently no more mind than he might the rattle of a passing truck. Ah, if he could but spot the devil of humour sparkling in Brian's eye! But no, he maintains I imagine it all, and Brian is simply too polite and restrained to take any offence at my antics.

Brian has a brother, Eamon. Curiously enough, if you sum their ages and add a further 18, you arrive at twice Brian's age, while if you subtract the age of the younger from the older and remove six from the difference, you arrive at Eamon's age. So, what age are the brothers?

ꟼNTUITION

LET US TALK, *MES AMIS*, ABOUT THE FEELINGS OF THE GUT.
The mind, it is quite sure that it understands the way that the world functions. Beneath the thoughts that you are aware of, the thoughts that you "hear" in your head, there are many more that never break the surface. They might warn you that someone is not to be trusted, or spur you on to turn left rather than right. They might lie to you shamelessly, without you ever knowing. It is not your fault. *C'est la vie!* It is important to know this.

So, engage your imagination for me once more – and this is not that last occasion! – but this time, picture you have a very thin, very large card. It is just four hundredths of an inch in thickness, one mere millimetre. You slice it into two halves, and place the two pieces upon each other, forming a very large, thin stack. Then you halve the stack and again double its height.

Now for once set aside your intuition and listen solely to mathematical logic. After a total of 52 such halvings and restackings, one for each card in a deck, how tall do you guess your stack to be?

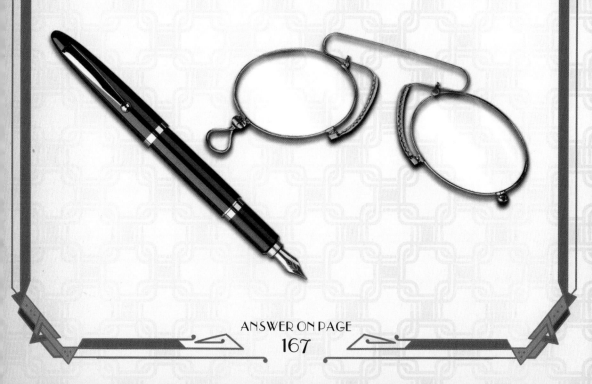

ANSWER ON PAGE
167

TRACK

ENGLAND IS A WINDING COUNTRY, FULL OF LITTLE TURNS AND CORNERS AND DIVERSIONS that seem to serve little purpose other than to befuddle the traveller and slow him down so that his progress is an interminable thing. The famously rolling and reeling road is a thing of antiquity, of history pressing itself into the future. Sometimes that is well and fine, of course. Then there are sometimes roads that are surprisingly straight – the legacy of Roman architects, unwilling to divert whenever possible to avoid. What was a forest, or a river, compared to the might of the Empire? Such determination was convenient for drivers, *certainement*, if not for road-diggers.

Hastings and I were on such a straight road, heading north out of London in his car. It was a pleasant day, and we were cruising at a comfortable 50 miles an hour when a lunatic sped past us, heading toward London in some fancy, multiple-cylindered thing at a speed of 80 miles an hour. We exchanged glances, and then Hastings demonstrated once again that curious turn of mind that so endears him to me by wondering how far apart our two cars would have been an hour ago.

I blinked, and asked if he imagined the two vehicles to be on perfectly straight tracks, and our speeds to have been invariant. He did not reply, but assuming those conditions, what would be the answer to his question?

DUBIOUS PROPOSITION

I WAS ONCE CORNERED BY A MAN WHO WAS *UN ESPÈCE D'IDIOT,* a particular fool. He had some political power in a small nation that I shall not identify, for fear of lowering your opinion of the place. Many powerful people seem to me to be disproportionately foolish. Such is the way of things, alas.

This fool suggested to me that he should enact a ban on sons – that is, once a woman had borne a male child, she should be forbidden from further issue. This simple fix – as if such a thing would be simple, *mon Dieu!* – would cut the rate of male births, providing a surplus of marriageable young women in the near future. I did not wait to hear why he thought such a thing to be beneficial, for my gorge had arisen, so I walked swiftly away.

I trust you can see why his insane plan would be an abject failure?

ANSWER ON PAGE
169

VOYAGE, VOYAGE

AH, TRAINS – SO UNPREDICTABLE! NOT A PLACE TO BE LOCKED IN WITH YOUR ENEMIES, I would suggest. On one journey, I had been travelling for an hour when the speed suddenly dropped to just 60 per cent of its former average. As a direct consequence of this, due, we were told, to problems of a mechanical nature, my arrival at my destination was two hours later than I had expected – a significant imposition.

The conductor was suitably shame-filled, although that was of little actual assistance. An unfortunate thing, for your job to require you to bear the guilt – and the ire of strangers – for things over which you have absolutely no influence. On the other hand, I did miss my luncheon, so I was not kindly disposed toward the fellow. The man informed me – rather oddly, I thought – that if the engines had malfunctioned 50 miles later, we would have arrived 40 minutes sooner.

That would still have been too late, but now, at least, you can tell me how many miles the voyage was?

ANSWER ON PAGE
170

SIDEWAYS

LOGICAL ADHERENCE TO THE FACTS DOES NOT IMPOSE A STRICTLY PEDESTRIAN approach to finding solutions. *Au contraire*! There are always times when the facts, as strictly verified, appear to point in one direction, or even to be ultimately self-contradictory. A narrow mind, one used only to thinking on familiar tracks, will find itself defeated by the weight of its own expectations. Try to cast aside the expected, *mes amis*, and allow the truth to shine through.

For example, let us say that you have, in front of you, three simple teacups of a typical design, and 10 individual pennies. Is it possible to place the pennies within the cups so that each cup contains an odd number of coins, with no pennies left over?

ANSWER ON PAGE
171

THE DISPLAY

I ONCE FOUND MYSELF IN THE UNENVIABLE SITUATION OF NEEDING TO RECONSTRUCT the precise disposition of an extremely complex floral arrangement dating to the previous summer. Everything hung on the orchids, you see. It so often does. Five ladies had contributed, each providing a different flower that had been grown, as it transpired, in a different country. The financial values of their contributions had similarly varied, regularly spanning the price range of three to seven shillings.

About Lucinda's contribution, I could discover little. For the others, however, I managed slightly better. Mary did not buy lilies. Nicolette's flowers cost a shilling less than the roses. Katherine paid more than the Belgian flowers cost. Amanda paid two shillings more than the French flowers cost. The French flowers cost five shillings, and were either tulips, or purchased by Mary. Of the chrysanthemums and tulips, I could say for certain that one cost four shillings, the other was purchased by Nicolette. The Dutch flowers were a shilling cheaper than the Belgian ones, and three shillings cheaper than the Spanish ones. The German flowers were not lilies.

So, who purchased the orchids, for how much, and from where did they originate?

ANSWER ON PAGE
172

CARSTAIRS

I WAS ALREADY AT CARSTAIRS WHEN THE LADY OF THE HOUSE, ELLEN TAIGHERTY, was murdered, one rainy afternoon. The formidable Dowager had been quite certain of her impending demise, hence the presence of Captain Hastings and myself. Alas that we were not swift enough to uncover the threat!

The details of Mrs Taigherty's murder were quite plain. She had been in a reading room, lost in a novel, when someone had come in through the garden door and stabbed her through the heart. Death would have been close to instantaneous. Her expression was one of mild annoyance, which was in accord with her usual manner.

The first person I spoke to after the murder was Mrs Taigherty's younger son, Shaun. I found him in the parlour, talking to his fiancée, Marian. There was friction between mother and wife-to-be, oh yes, so I enquired as to his movements since lunchtime. Shaun brushed away a damp forelock, looked me in the eye, and assured me with perfect sincerity that he had been in the parlour with Marian all afternoon. The young woman agreed with him immediately, and added they had been discussing various elements of the arrangements for their upcoming wedding until they learnt of the tragedy.

I wished the happy couple the very best of luck, and went off to find Hastings. Together, we waited for the local constabulary to arrive and once they did, I suggested they focus their attentions on Shaun as the most likely suspect. You see why?

GLOBAL

SOMETIMES, THE ANSWER TO A PROBLEM IS RIGHT IN THE FRONT OF THE FACE, but simply too close to see. It is necessary to take a step back, in order for the eyes to focus. Without such a movement, clear vision becomes highly obscured. So it is with some problems. You would not, I trust, stick your head deep into the lion's throat and then attempt to count the number of its teeth. Perspective is the vital key, *oui*?

There is a point from which you could look toward the North or the South of the planet, but not toward the East or the West.

Where do you imagine that is?

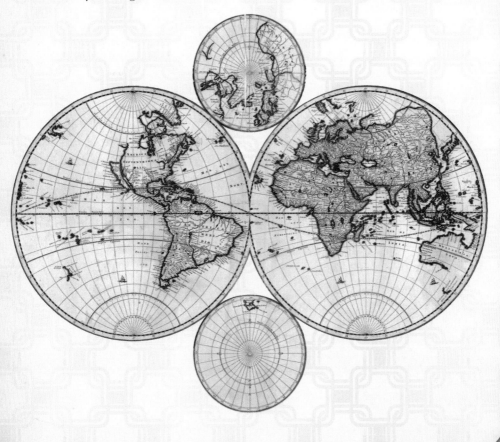

ANSWER ON PAGE
173

THE BICYCLE

Let us dare to suggest that you are in possession of a bicycle, my dear reader. I say this because Hercule Poirot and bicycles are not good friends, no, not at all! So, you, the bicycle, a companion, and an urgently required journey: this journey is 27 miles in length, quite the distance. You and your companion must set forth together and arrive together, as quickly as possible, with the aid of only the bicycle. That worthy steed will absolutely bear only one of you at a time.

Why is this happening to you? I'm sure a person of your ingenuity can think of a plausible reason. It would not happen to me, that is for certain, so I feel it is not for me to suppose a justification. So… You are a swift walker, at a reliable five miles per hour, one quarter faster than your companion. You are a slower cyclist, however, two miles per hour slower than your companion's ten. Your speeds will be constant, that is for sure, and your persons quite unmolested. Perhaps you are on Salisbury Plain, desperately attempting to reach the city at a coordinated moment.

How soon can you and your companion arrive at your destination?

DEUCTION

I never share an idea with Captain Hastings if it is unreliable.

I always dream about *crêpes*.

An idea is either a fact, or it is unreliable.

None of my ideas about *crêpes* are worth writing down.

I – eventually – share all of my facts with Captain Hastings.

If an idea of mine is unreliable, it is never accurate.

Captain Hastings is very fond of *crêpes*.

A dream is an idea.

Assume for a moment – if you will extend me such a kindness – that I have not gone quite mad, and yet all the above statements are accurate. Are my dreams factual?

ANSWER ON PAGE
175

THE THIN BLACK LINE

AH, THE PEN! MIGHTIER THAN THE SWORD, SO LONG AS YOU ARE NOT IN THE MIDDLE of a brutal medieval battle or hoping to hack down a bush of the brambles. The terror of the dictator. Collector's delight. Vital component of the humble squid. Friend and enemy of sheep everywhere. A powerful tool, yes, a powerful tool indeed.

Focus your little grey cells on the unlikely equation that reads 5+5+5+5=555. One single short stroke of your pen, if you have one, can turn that mathematical oddity into a perfectly valid sum.

Can you see how?

ANSWER ON PAGE
175

SOCIETAL

SOCIETY FUNCTIONS ARE A CURIOUS THING, MES AMIS. SO MANY PEOPLE, it seems to me, are terrified of their own company. They would readily submit to gatherings simply for the uncertain mercy of having the noise drown out the thoughts of their own interiors. It is a strangeness. And there are always some, primarily the predatory and unendurable, who come to mingle with those they resent simply to maintain status. As if not attending such a thing implies more than just "I was not present" – which, of course, it often does.

It is strange, *non*? Whimsical creatures, we are.

At a recent function, I had the displeasure of stumbling across several deeply flawed individuals. My purpose there was professional, of course. I shall inform you that either Leatherwood or Shropshire was insufferably narcissistic, that either Beeler, Rathbone or Shropshire was viciously sadistic, that either Leatherwood, Rathbone or Shropshire was prone to violent rage, and that either Beeler or Leatherwood was cretinous to the point where I wondered that the man was able to remember to keep drawing breath. You shall inform me which man was which, yes?

ANSWER ON PAGE
176

REPLICATION

IT IS OF CRUCIAL IMPORTANCE TO UNDERSTAND THE PRECISE IMPLICATIONS OF THE SCIENTIFIC PROCESS. The methodical and rigorous analysis of information is the stone at the corner of our modern world. We have moulded the earth to our whims through our mastery of fact. It is our greatest strength, and should be accorded suitable reverence.

Let us say that you, clever person that you are, have examined a set of facts, and have formulated a theory. Assessing it with a critical eye, you think that you are 90 per cent certain that you are correct. But you do not wish to be complacent, and because the spirit of science burns within you, you enlist several entirely independent colleagues to also evaluate the likelihood of your theory.

So, you pass your facts to four others, and each one assesses the theory on his or her own, without cross-reference. Soon, you have their replies, and each agrees with you precisely. This leaves you with five assessments, each one placing your theory's likelihood of being correct at 90 per cent.

What is the chance that the theory is correct?

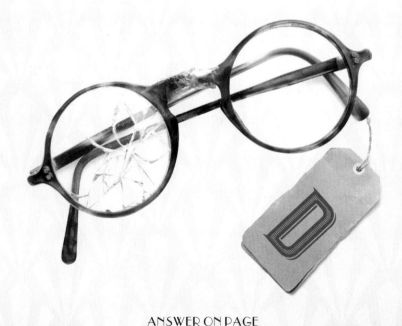

ANSWER ON PAGE
177

ℒIARS, ℒIARS

WHEN IT COMES TO UNPICKING TRUTH FROM FICTION, WITNESSES ARE OFTEN of critical importance. This is not news to you, I am quite certain. But even with the best will in the world, such people are often highly unreliable. And then of course there may be the criminal and his or her accomplices. They will naturally be strongly motivated to mislead. But there is always a truth behind the stories, and to find its shape, one needs only to gather sufficient reliable information. So, in the statements that come from those surrounding a crime, often the matter reduces down to a calculus of honesty.

An illustration is in order, *n'est-ce pas*? Let us posit three people, with three stories. Person X tells us, among other things, that person Y is lying. Person Y tells us person Z is lying, while person Z tells us both X and Y are lying. If one of the three is telling us the truth, which one must it be?

ANSWER ON PAGE
178

FATHER

THE WAYS OF THE RUSTIC FOLK OF YOUR ENGLISH COUNTRYSIDE OFTEN SEEM a little strange to Hercule Poirot, as indeed must my ways to them. The ubiquity of tea as a breakfast drink is something quite baffling to me, for example. How can you hope to fortify yourself for a day with such a thin beverage? Where is the fuel to get the little grey cells working? *Quelle horreur!* But although I do not understand, I accept. It is your style. I likewise extend my acceptance to every innocent *eccentricté*, and can only hope fondly for my own peculiarities to be likewise benevolently met.

Last Thursday, I was introduced to a Lady Cornelia Tassiter, who informed me without the slightest hint of embarrassment or jocularity that her father was older than her grandfather. A lesser man might have blanched at such a suggestion, or comported himself with unseemly doubt, but not Hercule Poirot, oh no! I took the pronouncement in my pace, without falter. In fact, I quickly ascertained that she was merely reporting mundane fact. You see how, I assume?

ANSWER ON PAGE
179

THE WHEEL

I HAVE REFERRED ELSEWHERE TO MY DIFFICULT RELATIONSHIP WITH THE BICYCLE. It is not that I despise the machine, not at all. *Au contraire*, I have the greatest respect for the device. It permits millions of people a mobility of freedom, while helping to rescue the city from the tyranny of horse-stench. Also, it is significantly less expensive to maintain than either a horse or a motorcar. It requires a significant outlay of muscular energy as well – energy far better saved for cogitation, but in that it is no more distasteful than falling back upon the Ponies of Shank.

Even with all that said, the bicycle is not for Hercule Poirot, unless the very direst needs require. One fellow's meat is another person's toxin, *oui*? Consider, for example, the bicycle in motion as it is steered down a slope. The top of the wheel is moving forward at the same rate as the bottom of the wheel, *oui*?

BLACK HAT

LET US TURN ONCE MORE TO THE MIGHTY ENGINE OF WONDER THAT IS your collected imaginations, my friends. *C'est vrai*, I place much importance on that faculty for the purposes of the instruction. How else is one to arrange the appropriate circumstances, without endless supplies of time, patience, and willing helpers? Here is a subtle truth for you: deep down, the mind cannot see the difference between imagination and reality, your world is constructed by the little grey cells, from the inputs of your senses. Imagination is the same thing, except the inputs come from the self. So, imagination is reality – at least until you try to eat it, of course.

So, you are at the front of a line of three people. Each of you is wearing one hat of five. Those five consist of three black and two white hats, but you do not know which hat you have been given. You may only look forward, and speak only as directed. Your two companions are in identical situations, and every bit as logically deft as you are. Your examiner, who placed the hats, asks the person at the back the colour of their own hat. "I don't know," is the reply. Then the middle person is asked, and gives the same reply.

So, what colour is your own hat?

ANSWER ON PAGE
180

THE MIRACLES OF BIRTH

AH, PROBABILITY! OF ALL OF THE BRANCHES OF THE MATHEMATICAL ARTS, is there any that so regularly confounds the expectations born of the experience of daily life? A detective should not deal in probabilities, of course. One should restrict oneself to absolute facts. If 19 times out of 20 it is the butler who needs arrest, this is insufficient to destroy an innocent man's life. But for all that, the art of probability remains useful in assessing which risks and outcomes are worth chancing, and which are not. Evidence, it is not, but it remains a valuable tool nonetheless.

So, pray consider a trifling issue for a moment. A husband and wife have four children of differing ages. Presuming there is no biological disposition either way, do you think they are more likely to have three children of one gender and one of the other, or two children of each?

ANSWER ON PAGE

181

A SIMPLE MATTER

THERE'S NO NEED TO EXERCISE YOUR POOR, WEARY IMAGINATIONS THIS TIME, *mes amis*. The following 12 words can be divided into four categories of three words each. Specifically, these are birds, colours, minerals, and poisoner's fruits. It will be a matter of a few instants to sort the 12 into the correct groups, surely?

BORAX
CORDOVAN
GRULLO
HOATZIN
JACAMAR
MANCHINEEL
NOSEAN
SPINDLE
TALC
TINAMOU
WAHOO
WENGE

ANSWER ON PAGE
181

THE SECOND DEDUCTION

Nothing that has been well polished
could possibly be undesirable.

Nothing with a bell is ever quite quiet.

Everything that is not undesirable could
be housed in my living room.

Bicycles are always given signals.

Nothing could be housed in my living room that is not quiet.

Anything given signals is fitted with a bell.

As before, please favour me with your assumption of sanity, and treat the above series of unlikely statements as accurate. From them, can you then decide whether a bicycle can ever be well polished?

ANSWER ON PAGE
182

ECCENTRICITIES

CONSIDER IF YOU WILL, FIVE HYPOTHETICALLY FUSSY INDIVIDUALS WHO ARE possessed of quite strong feelings regarding the geographical surroundings in which they find themselves. To the untrained eye these preferences may appear quite arbitrary, but that is not the case, oh no!

Roisin Harley likes swamps, but dislikes plateaus. Thomas Masters likes mountains, but dislikes tundra. Geoffrey Fielding likes forests, but dislikes the bayou. Ralph Pullins likes plains, but dislikes badlands. So, which does Corinne Rhodes prefer, taigas or islands?

ANSWER ON PAGE
182

CAROLINGIANS

OUR ANCIENT ANCESTORS WERE MOST CERTAINLY OF A SUPERSTITIOUS NATURE. It is inevitable, *non*? The knowledge that we have now, it was not there. Lacking understanding, the curious mind turns to fancies. An event happens, a correlation is observed. It happens again, and a belief formed. Then, if the correlation later fails... Well, that is surely the fault of the believer, not of the belief. Perhaps it only works when one is carrying a sheaf of wheat, as one was the last time. From such tangled messes are superstitions born.

Such a fable arose I am told, at the court of King Charles le Magne. Many and varied were the wise councillors accreted around that worthy's throne, like a pearl surrounding an irritant in an oyster. Eventually, it became obvious that their numbers would have to be thinned. But superstition dictated specific requirements of councillors that had to be met, lest the angelic hosts look on the King with disfavour.

Three deaf advisors were required, along with three blind, three mute, and three lacking thumbs, so that between them all, the various worldly blandishments could be resisted. There had to be three advisors who were totally bald, three who had long beards, and three who were clean-shaven, that the breadth of human experience be encompassed. Finally, there needed to be three men and three women to provide balance.

To obey the dictates of iron superstition, how few councillors could Charles le Magne get away with retaining?

ANSWER ON PAGE
183

THE CART

THERE HAS BEEN MUCH MADE, OVER THE YEARS, OF THE CROSSING OF THE RIVER with the cabbages and the goat and the wolf, and perhaps the scorpion and several highly chaste sisters as well. Now, Hercule Poirot is not shy of the hypothetical situation, particularly as a means of exciting the little grey cells. But perhaps it is not always necessary to leap merrily toward the abstraction, *n'est-ce pas*? The hypothetical does not always mean the impractical.

So, let us return to our clever Yorkshire bishop of times past for another exercise. There is a boat, of very dubious quality, and a fast river, likewise. A family – a father, a mother and two sons under the age of seven – desires crossing, but the boat can only safely bear the weight of one adult. So, how are they all to cross?

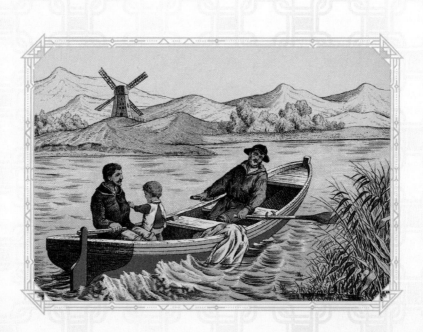

ANSWER ON PAGE
183

ꝘHE COST OF ꝘIVING

AH, MODERN LIFE IS SO EXPENSIVE, *N'EST-CE PAS?*
SOMETIMES IT SEEMS AS IF one has to merely walk out of the door
to find one's purse hollowed out, seemingly as if by the powers of magic! The
truth, of course, is less fanciful. For the unwary, the mind does not pay too much
attention to the little moments of transaction here and there. As a result, we are
left wondering what has happened, when the truth is that there was a multitude
of little moments.

Permit me to describe for you my day, yesterday. To make matters less taxing,
I shall convert the peculiar maze of British coins and notes into simply pence.
After breakfast, Hastings and I went to Marble Arch, to observe a particular
individual at the Speakers' Corner in Hyde Park. Along the way, I purchased
a newspaper for two pence, and sacrificed six pence to a rather fey young man
for a copy of his folio of poetry. We then took a cab to central Croydon, which
required half of the money I had. There we met with an old and dear friend in a
rather good pub, and had lunch, which cost me 20 pence.

From there we went to a crumbling bookshop, and I purchased a very curious
volume supposedly translated from Arabic, which took half of my remaining
funds, and earned me a peculiar look from the equally crumbling bookseller. We
returned to Waterloo by train, at a cost of 12 pence, and finally, three-quarters of
my now-depleted money was required to see me returned home. I gave my last
sixpence to a homeless woman almost on my doorstep.

How much did I leave home with?

LUGGAGE

FROM THE PRACTICALITIES OF THE REAL SWIFTLY BACK TO THE INTANGIBLE AND HYPOTHETICAL, *mes amis*. Imagine five large trunks of luggage. It may be for the best to imagine them as being identical in all significant particulars, for they are metaphorical in broad intent, and it would not be helpful in this particular endeavour to become distracted with meditations upon the various styles now common in travel equipment. So, five pieces of luggage…

Now, let us further consider that the five pieces of luggage are being sent from London to five different destinations – specifically, Blackpool, Cork, Coventry, Truro, and Whitby. So, which of these five locations is least like the others? The answer is not a trick of language.

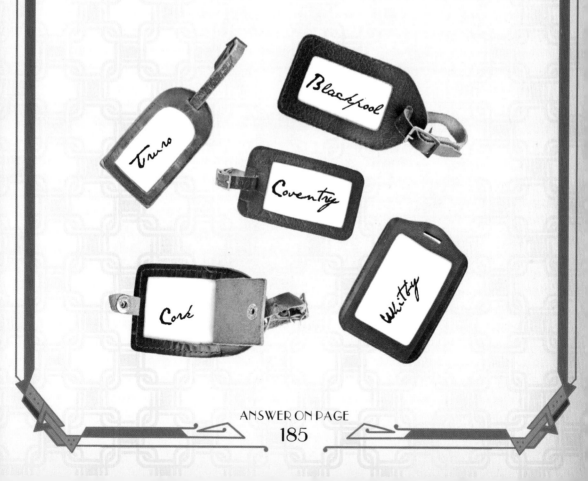

ANSWER ON PAGE
185

FRUIT

HAVE YOU CONSIDERED A CURRENCY OF FRUIT, *MES AMIS*? I SUSPECT YOU HAVE NOT. I suspect that the unwieldy nature of large amounts of fruit – and its transience, in terms of both its propensity to decay over time and its relative ease of damage – would put significant downward pressures on the accumulation of large amounts of fruit-wealth. Particularly if it was decided that frozen or otherwise preserved fruit lost an amount of their value. Whether this pressure might be a good thing or a bad thing is left as an exercise to those gifted in economic analysis.

I ask not merely out of idle fancy, but due to a conversation I had yesterday with a small boy. "Six plums and an apple are worth one pear," he told me, with perfect seriousness. I expressed my gratitude for the information. He nodded, my thanks clearly his anticipated dues. "Three apples and a pear are worth 10 plums," he added confidentially. Then he scampered away, muttering something about grapes. I feel that he is in danger of ending up as a writer in his adulthood, the poor lad.

Still, you can inform me of the relative values of apples to pears, *oui*?

A SIMPLE LITTLE LIST

A MATTER PURELY TO GIVE THE LITTLE GREY CELLS SOME EXERCISE, *MES AMIS*. If you were to select an answer entirely at random from the short list below, what is the probability that the answer you pick will be the correct answer to this question?

A: 25 per cent
B: 50 per cent
C: 0 per cent
D: 25 per cent.

STAFFORD

ON THE AFTERNOON THAT RUDOLPH STAFFORD WAS MURDERED, A NUMBER OF PEOPLE had assembled at his son's home for Sunday luncheon. After a reportedly pleasant meal, the assorted dinner guests had split into smaller groups, and busied themselves at various pursuits – croquet, reading, tippling, and things of that nature. Rudolph had taken himself off for a little snooze, which then proved fatal.

There was nothing in the manner of death – stabbing – to rule out any suspect. However, just three of the people at Edward Stafford's house spent sufficient time out of the company of their fellow guests during the pertinent period. I spoke to them all, *naturallement*, to ascertain with what they had been engaging themselves during the suspicious interlude.

Edward Stafford, spotting the postman in the lane that the estate was on, had wandered down to the gatehouse to see if an expected missive from a cousin in Venice had been delivered. Alas, it had not. Katherine Moody, Edward's sister, had been in the rose garden, taking a chance to escape, for a moment of tranquillity, the burdens of motherhood. Leon Godfrey, Edward's friend and business partner, snuck into the library to peruse one of Edward's books that he had long admired, a rather splendid first edition of Carroll's *Alice*.

The culprit is obvious, *oui*?

ANSWER ON PAGE
187

THE HOSPITAL

BEFORE THE GREAT WAR, I WORKED IN BRUSSELS, AS THE CHIEF OF THE POLICE FORCES there. When the enemy invaded, and the rape of my poor homeland began, I fled to England. I did not arrive unscathed – I limped rather piteously, for a while – but I was infinitely more fortunate than many others, a fact that I shall never forget.

The hospital in Ghent, where I was made fit to continue, was a sight I shall always carry with me. *Quelle horreur*! Is it any wonder even now, I will always set myself against the perpetrator of violence and cruelty? In one ward alone, there were 43 missing legs, 38 ruined hands, 35 blinded in at least one eye, and 33 deafened.

Supposing those injuries were as evenly distributed as possible, and that two terrible unfortunates had suffered all four atrocities, you can of course tell me how many men the ward held. *Oui*?

ANSWER ON PAGE
188

ESSENTIAL KNOWLEDGE

WE ALL HAVE A LITTLE – OR NOT SO LITTLE – SUPPLY OF ESSENTIAL KNOWLEDGE, things that we have learned to be true and reliable through repeated experiences and teachings. Those things are so obvious to us that we rarely think about them. Most of these items are firmly true for the large amount of the times, of course. If this were not so, we would be completely unable to function in the world. Our expectations would be confounded at every turn, *oui*?

But for the detective, who relies on clear understanding, it is vitally important to know *why* our expectations are true. If we know that ice is only slippery because of the water it produces when our footsteps put pressure on it, we will know that in unusually extreme cold, it is no more slippery than rock. Perhaps an alibi hangs on not being able to walk quickly on a long stretch of ice, hmmm…?

Think. Question. Do not assume. This is the path to accurate understanding. So, what shape is water?

ANSWER ON PAGE
188

ᕲOGMATIC

KEEP FAITH, *MES AMIS!* RECENTLY, A FRIEND OF MINE, JACK TARRANT, eloped with the daughter of a curate, one Rose Aldred. Jack always has been charming and sweet-natured, I feel, but his father is a weaver, and old Aldred had hopes she would be a very good catch for someone higher on the social ladder, yes? Ah, but those possessed of youth are passionate in love! Paternal whim is not territory I have great knowledge of, but life must be lived as you see fit, or cares and regrets will be your lot.

The father is still apoplectic. "Rabble" is how he describes his son-in-law, I hear. Such a barb is only going to exacerbate his heaped problems, though. As the Bard would say, it causes much ado, vexation of this sort. Jack has already smartened up under Rose's care, and despite her father's disavowal, I only foresee advancement for the pair. Her heart is true, as is his. Eventually, the curate's wrath will dispel, and all snide eruptions be forgiven.

Vexatious as events are for Rose and Jack, my purpose here is not to overwhelm you, my friend, with personal esoterica. Melded within the letters comprising this tale are the names of several creatures. How many different ones can you find? Remember, it is – though naturally uncommon – key to develop the facility to look past distractions.

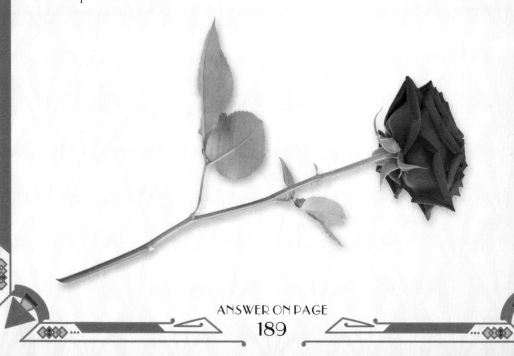

ANSWER ON PAGE
189

MENTAL JUGGLING

SOMETIMES, FOR THE DETECTIVE, IT IS ADVANTAGEOUS TO HOLD THE MENTAL FLEXIBILITY required to work a chain of deductions through to their logical conclusion. This is obvious, *oui*? To that worthy end, I propose the following exercise.

There is a number I am considering. It holds the property that when it is quadrupled, then this product increased by three quarters, the result being singly incremented and then divided by nine, two being added to this quotient, the result being doubled, this sum then being multiplied by itself, the resulting square being cut to one hundredth of itself, seven being removed afterwards, the square root then being taken of the remaining difference, this root being increased by two, results in the number five?

FRENCH GOODS

IT WAS DENNIS TAFT WHO STUMBLED ACROSS THE BODY OF REGINALD SHAW late one night. I mean that in the literal way, as Monsieur Taft shakily reported actually tripping over Monsieur Shaw's corpse in the dark of Shaw's office. Both men worked at Black's French Goods. As Monsieur Taft was heading home for the night, he noticed the door to Shaw's office was ajar. Through the crack, it was obvious to him that some disturbance had taken place in the room. Naturally, he was concerned, and decided to investigate further, whereupon he made his unfortunate discovery. Ah, but no good deed goes unpunished, *n'est-ce pas?*

Enquiring into the affairs of the company, I found a number of eccentricities and oddities. There were financial uncertainties, depleted bank coffers, thin order books, and enough recriminations to provide fuel for a dozen blood feuds in less civilized corners of the world. Perhaps the surprise then was not that someone had died, but that someone had not died sooner. To me it was obvious that Taft was the murderer, of course. I trust you understand my thoughts?

ANSWER ON PAGE

190

ANOTHER CIPHER

I HAVE SPOKEN EARLIER ON THE OCCASIONAL TENDENCY FOR THE CRIMINAL TO ATTEMPT the hiding of fact with codes and ciphers. Truly, we are fortunate that such endeavours are hasty and ill-conceived, *généralement*.

In the spirit of such things, I thus offer you another sample for your enlightenment, *mes amis*. It is not encrypted in precisely the same way as my previous example, and rather than districts of London, it is the names of politicians that I have prepared.

What are they?

```
WALRA   NOBWE   RDNAE
GROEG   DYOLL   DIVAD
HTIUQ   SAYRN   EHTRE
BREHN   AMREN   NABLL
EBPMA   CYRNE   HRUOF
    LABRU   HTRA
```

RITUAL

AH, THE VAGARIES OF THE SOCIAL RITUAL! WE TEND TO NATURALLY ASSUME THAT the cultural habits we are familiar with are the ones that are universal, of course. A moment's thought should make it clear that they are nothing of the sort. Why, even in such a short distance as lies between Belgium and Britain, such a common act as greeting changes its very nature.

As suits the British reserve – ah, the famous fear of emotion and its display, leading to so many of the peculiarities of your national psyche – a greeting is a firm, short handshake, conducted at as long a distance as is unobtrusively practical. In Brussels, one places the hand lightly on the other's arm, and three swift kisses are offered, past one side of the face, then the other, and then back to the first. Do not try such a conviviality in London, *mes amis*!

Still, the handshake is a noble enough undertaking. It is clear and obvious that there must be a certain amount of *personnes* who have shaken hands with an odd number of other people. Do you suppose this amount of persons to be odd, even, or impossible to determine?

ANSWER ON PAGE
191

BLESSINGS

IN THE HYPOTHETICAL REALMS THAT EXIST TO SERVE THE NEED OF PLACING CONUNDRUMS into a recognizable context – and many they are, my friend, as you know all too well – it is not just the young who bedevil the old with convoluted reasoning. I shall demonstrate. You, being the fine and insightful person you are, would expect nothing less, I am certain.

So, we have an old man, and a young boy. Perhaps they are grandfather and grandson, sitting on a wooden bench under an oak tree, enjoying a sunny afternoon. Yes, let us assume that. The grandfather looks over at the grandson, and says, "Live as long again as you have already, and then all the same over again, and then three times as much as everything to that point, and take one of my years besides to call your own, then, my lad, you will live a whole century."

The boy, I suspect, replies with a statement such as, "You're funny, grandpa," but in the meanwhile, you can tell me the age of the boy, *oui*?

ANCESTRY

I AM WELL AWARE THAT I HAVE ALREADY SHARED MY OPINIONS REGARDING the dangers of the intuitions with you, *mes amis*. It is so very important to understand, however. The world of the reality is not the shape that we believe it to be. For much of the time the differences do not matter, it is true. The change is so meagre that it would not feed even a mouse. But if you want to truly understand the reasons why things are as they are, or to uncover the truth of a devious criminal act, you need to set aside your presumptions.

Do not do that just now. Yes, I know, but I seek an illustration for you. So take a quick guess, and tell me, how many ancestors – direct ones only, parents of parents of parents and so on – do you think you have had in total over the last 500 years?

A TRIAL

THE FOLLOWING LITTLE TRIAL I OFFERED TO HASTINGS ONE QUIET AFTERNOON, as a test of his ingenuity. He seemed a little put out, but did eventually agree to attempt a solution. After a period of time, he managed to find one. I think he was not entirely happy with me, but he did better than I had feared that he might. Ah, but a little exercise is a very fine thing for the grey cells, yes? But of course, you agree. Why else would you be here, after all?

So, what I wish for you to do is to write down seven odd digits that sum to 18. Trivial, yes?

FINE ALE

IMAGINE, *MES AMIS*, YOU ARE INDIVIDUALLY WANDERING THROUGH THE RURAL COUNTRYSIDE. I know not what dire manner of the situation provoked this need, but alas, such things do happen in even the most blessed of lives, *oui*? Let us say, for the sake of clear mental images, that you are within the county of Hookland, making your way from Holdhurt Row to the village of Hobble. Perhaps you are in desperate need of a pint of Hicks Breweries' famous *Toad in the Bottle*, or Sutherland's equally excellent *Old Clip*. That would at least make firm sense.

So, you are between hamlets, navigating the winding country walkways, and come to the junction known as Crooked Cross, where dread Tanglefoot himself is said to lurk, come dark. The wooden signpost and its markers point the way to Hobble and Holdhurt Row, and also to Burr Hill, Lark Hill, Cob Castle, Whitebarrow Hill and Marshwood Vale. Alas, the signpost has blown down, and while it is otherwise unharmed, without a map you are quite clueless as to which of seven paths will take you on toward Hobble.

What are you to do?

THE KILLER

A VERY SIMPLE LITTLE MATTER THIS WOULD BE FOR ALL, WERE YOU THERE IN THE ROOM IN QUESTION. As it is, it is still a very simple little matter for some. Ah, but perhaps I indulge my thoughts a little too much! Every question is simple when you know the answer, *n'est-ce pas?*

Alors! There are four people in a room, pillars of the local community – a lawyer, a doctor, a business executive, and a scientist. You know that they hold these career positions, but not who fills which role. In fact, you know absolutely nothing else about these worthies – save that one is a killer, and that this man's first name is Brian. Despite your comparative ignorance, you are able to look into the room and wordlessly identify the murderer. How so?

PIGS

LET US SURMISE, MY FRIENDS, THAT YOU HAVE BECOME ACQUAINTED WITH A YOUNG MAN of rural Hookland, who has recently inherited a portion of his father's herd of swine. Perhaps you fall to talking with him in the curious village of Hobble, over the pint of Old Clip you so tenaciously sought.

Tom, for such is his name, is the middle brother of three. His older brother, Will, was left precisely 25 per cent more pigs than his younger brother, Ed, and 20 per cent more than Tom himself received. It is still the custom, in such parts of the country, for a trace of primogeniture to remain, and neither Tom nor Ed feel slighted. "Tis only proper," Tom declares.

When Tom informs you that his share of the livestock amounts to a pleasingly rounded – and impressively prosperous – 1,000 pigs, I am sure that you can inform me how many swine Ed obtained, yes?

ANSWER ON PAGE
194

STICKY

I WISH YOU TO IMAGINE A PIECE OF WOOD. ALLOW ME TO SUGGEST THAT IT BE a smallish branch, fallen from some unfortunate tree. It is leafless, so perhaps it is winter, or it has been separated from its tree for some time. The branch is maybe a couple of pounds in weight, and a couple of feet in length. It is not insignificant, this branch, but neither would it make a useful weapon in any but the most trivial – or utterly desperate – circumstances. In this, it is not unique. In fact, this is the very essence of the thing. The branch is ordinary, unremarkable, much like any of a thousand others you would find within a modest patch of forest.

You take the branch in your hand, and with all the strength available to you, throw it away from yourself. It zooms off to a respectable distance, but it is slowing steadily, and eventually it comes to a complete halt. Having done so, it starts returning to you. Before long, it comes straight back to your hand with a noticeable thwack. At no point did the branch bounce, ricochet or deflect off anything. Its journey was undisturbed. It is not cunningly curved. You did not affix any string, elastic, or other thing to it before throwing.

So tell me, *mes amis*. What happened?

WORKING UP HIGH

AH, THE HYPOTHETICAL! WHERE WOULD I BE WITHOUT IT, IN SITUATIONS such as this? *Certainement*, cogitation is one of humanity's greatest gifts. It is of critical importance to the detective, always. How else is one to examine a set of facts and attempt to knit them into a theory, if not by considering all the hypothetical possibilities that might fit? There is no other way known to Hercule Poirot, this much is certain.

So, let us conjure a hypothetical fellow, working at his lofty office building, ten stories above the ground. In an unguarded moment, he is startled by some threat – such as a particularly aggressive and generously sized wasp, for example – and, caught out, leaps straight through the floor-to-ceiling window that he is standing next to. The sides of the building are quite sheer, and in the moment of leaping, the man's hands are fully occupied with fending off his assailant. However, when all is resolved, the man is fired from his job, otherwise unharmed by his ordeal. How is this so?

ANSWER ON PAGE
195

CLIFF

THE TRAGIC DEATH OF NATHAN STOTT WAS WIDELY REPORTED IN THE NATIONAL PRESS. Along with a friend, Victor Grant, Nathan and his brother Isaac were spending a day climbing at the local *escarpement*. Alas, the guide rope snapped while Nathan was abseiling down, and he fell! Isaac, who had been addressing their picnic, came running to find his brother broken on top of the heaped rope that should have been Nathan's support, with Victor up above, at the cliff's edge, wailing in horror.

The papers, of course, were quick to seize on the story, and Victor was even persuaded to speak tearfully of his horror as he realized the rope was snapping up by the cliff's edge. He was quite powerless to do anything but yell wordlessly before it gave, taking his dangling friend with it. Isaac, in turn, spoke movingly of his brother's kindness, and his devastation at Nathan's death.

Having read the articles, I wasted little time in penning a note to the local constabulary that Nathan was most certainly murdered. You see why, I trust?

ANSWER ON PAGE
194

A LEISURELY VOYAGE

IT IS USUALLY NOT WORTH THE TROUBLE TO EXERT ONESELF WITH TRIPS HERE AND THERE, scurrying back and forth like a busy little mouse. The true detective, everything he or she needs is within the facts, and the facts better catalogued by others. Besides, walking around uses up the time of the day so very quickly: it is not useful.

An illustration is useful, *n'est-ce pas*? But of course it is. So… Somehow, you decide that it is useful to walk to a place a mile away. Perhaps they serve an excellent brandy. You arrive there in a relaxed 20 minutes, and enjoy your brandy. How quickly would you need to walk on your return journey to bring your average walking speed for the trip to a reasonable six miles an hour?

EASTBOURNE

HASTINGS AND I WERE IN EASTBOURNE ONE AFTERNOON, ENGAGED IN A RATHER CURIOUS business involving a magnificently carved stone bust, some powder of uncertain origin, and an unexpected tunnel. It was a nasty affair, *mes amis*. But at the moment of which I am thinking, I was sitting on a pleasantly shaded bench beside the road, watching the approach of Hastings from a way down the road.

As he walked toward me, he was slowly catching up with a tractor, which was pulling a large tree trunk behind it. He paid the tree no mind, and eventually passed it, no more than 10 feet from arriving at my bench. I waited a moment then sharply told him to walk back the way he had come. He eyed me for a moment and then obeyed. Thanks to his timely efforts, I was able to see that while it took him 70 paces to walk past the tree toward me, he required only 10 to walk its length when going in the other direction.

I called him back, and thanked him for his exquisite assistance. Since dear Hastings had not been in any particular hurry, the length of his pace was about a foot. We shall presume that to be exact, and, so presuming, can you tell me the length of the tree trunk?

ANSWER ON PAGE
198

FACTS

WITH ENOUGH FACTS, THE TRUTH OF A SITUATION MUST BECOME CLEAR. This is simply obvious, I am sure. The genius of Hercule Poirot lies in my being able to assemble the correct picture from the smallest basket of facts, rather than the whole pile. Without any facts, however, I would be quite as lost as anybody else.

So, let me confide in you, *mes amis*. It is an indisputable fact that party, infill, fire, knee, and pony are all varieties of a certain physical thing. What is that thing?

TRUTH

IN A MOMENT, I WILL PRESENT YOU WITH A STATEMENT THAT EXTENDS ACROSS SEVERAL LINES. Your task is to ensure that the statement is correct. You will easily spot some blank, underlined spaces within the statement. These are your vessel for correcting the statement. In each, you are to enter a number, using only the digits zero to nine. This is very simple, yes? Ah, but the execution, she may prove a little more troublesome!

Alors! The statement is as follows.

The five following lines include:

___ uses of the digit 1,

___ uses of the digit 2,

___ uses of the digit 3,

___ uses of the digit 4, and

___ uses of the digit 5.

You can fill in the blanks above to make the statement true, yes?

CAT AND MOUSE

LET US HYPOTHESIZE THAT THERE IS AN INDUSTRIOUS MOUSE THAT HAS CHEWED A ROW of no less than five holes in your lovely new wainscoting. These holes are, of course, interconnected. Infuriated, you take firm hold of your cat – you *do* have a cat, don't you? – and instruct him or her to solve your mouse problem. The cat, of course, ignores you, but after several rounds of wheedling, bribery and begging on your part, finally agrees to assist.

The cat is faced with five holes to search for the mouse. The mouse can be in any one of them. After the cat unsuccessfully searches a hole, it withdraws and pauses for a moment to take stock, during which time the mouse nervously runs to an adjacent hole.

If the cat is clever enough to use the best technique – and, of course, it is – then what is the greatest number of searches it will have to make to catch the mouse?

DRURY LANE

SIR WINFORTH HEPWOOD, MP WAS MAKING USE OF THE GENTLEMAN'S FACILITIES during a performance at the Theatre Royal on Drury Lane, London, when some rapscallion attempted to murder him. Most unseemly! Sir Hepwood, the Member of Parliament for Coreham, was in the process of tidying his moustache at the sinks when a stall burst open right behind him (you may remember the affair from the newspapers). A darkly clad fellow appeared, fired at him, and vanished out of the lavatory before Sir Hepwood could recover from his frozen terror. Fortunately, the bullet whistled over the honourable MP's shoulder, and all was well.

Hastings and I were called to examine the untouched scene early the next morning, as Inspector Japp was under considerable pressure to ensure that the matter was swiftly resolved. Normally, I would not venture forth, but I had some mild curiosity about the site of the attack. We found the lavatory in the sort of perfect order you'd expect from the Theatre Royal, were shown the cavernous sink and equally expansive mirror Sir Hepwood had been using, glanced over the perfidious stall, and took our leave again.

Later, I informed the good Japp – to his great displeasure and mistrust – that his honourable politician was an arrant liar, and there was no case to investigate. You can see why, I trust?

ANSWER ON PAGE
200

LUMBERING

FOR A MOMENT, LEND YOUR LITTLE GREY CELLS TO THE HUMBLE WOODSMAN. If there is an arrogant woodsman – as surely there must be, somewhere – he plays no further part in this matter. Move on! Now, splitting trees into firewood is a rugged task for rugged people, make no mistake. Hercule Poirot would be a most unsatisfactory woodsman, *mais oui*, although perhaps Captain Hastings would find the work invigorating.

So we have a woodsman, humble and rugged, and he has a companion, also a woodsman, equally humble and rugged. In one day of work, this doughty pair can cut 150 cubic metres of logs into firewood, or 100 cubic metres of tree trunk into logs. Armed with this startlingly impressive information, you will of course be able to inform me how many metres of trunk they should log in the morning in order to be able to finish splitting all of those same logs precisely by the end of the working day. Yes?

MONK

THERE IS A MONASTERY, AT THE EDGE OF AN ISOLATED RANGE OF HILLS. That is a suitable location for a monastery, *non*? It seems to Hercule Poirot that the most effective way to think about the divine is to escape the clutching tendrils of the temporal. A monastery in the heart of a bustling city must, of needs, be at something of a disadvantage, at least in terms of its spiritual output.

Our monastery contains 12 monks – three of them lectors, four serving as deacons, and the remaining five priests. Upon receiving a basket of apples, a gross plus two score in total, the monks decide to distribute fruit with but a modest weighting according to station. The priests are to get slightly more apples than the deacons, and the lectors slightly less, the amount of difference to that number being received by the deacons being the same in both cases. Knowing that the deacons and lectors are to share one less than a hundred apples, you can tell me how many pieces of fruit each lector received, *oui*?

ANSWER ON PAGE
202

COURTYARD

I KNOW OF A COURTYARD DEEP INSIDE THE GROUNDS OF AN ANCIENT UNIVERSITY COLLEGE, one which for centuries has been turning out merrily drunken students, and will, I assume, continue to do so for centuries more. Many things change as the years turn – *mon Dieu*, how they turn! – but the drinking habits of students do not appear to be variable.

Now, this courtyard is surrounded on all four sides by small apartments, occupied by said students. Each wall has 20 openings, equally spaced, and the doors to the apartments are numbered clockwise from 1 to 80, starting at the southwest corner. Number 13 is not an apartment, but the number given to the tunnel that leads out onto the rest of the campus, and of course there are no doors placed in corners. Naturally, apartments 12 and 14 are highly prized for their convenience, but also very noisy.

We, however, are concerned with apartments 9, 25, 52, and 73, each of which is on a different wall of the courtyard. These apartments are held by a group of friends. From which of these four doors is the combined direct distance to the other three the shortest? For the sake of ease, let us pretend that the large, battle-scarred oak tree in the centre of the courtyard does not exist.

ANSWER ON PAGE
203

MISCREANTS

LET US SUPPOSE THAT YOU ARE FACED WITH A TRIO OF POSSIBLE MISCREANTS. These things happen, particularly if you are a parent or a detective. Hercule Poirot is one of these things, but not the other, thank the Lord himself. Parenthood requires many wonderful qualities, some of which I am perhaps not in the greatest supply of. My attentions are elsewhere, *n'est-ce pas?*

Of your three miscreants, you are aware that one of them will always lie to you, one will always tell you the truth, and one will do either according to whim. Alas, you do not know which is which, and when they lie, they do so perfectly, without any indication. So you attempt to find out which is the one you can trust.

The first tells you that the second is the truthful one. The second tells you that the first is not the liar. The third does not answer your question, but tells you that if your question had been about the identity of the whimsical person, who both lies and tells the truth, your answer would have been it is the second person who is whimsical.

Which of the three can you rely on to always tell you the truth?

THE COUNTRYSIDE

THE BUCOLIC LIFESTYLE IS NOT FOR ME, *MES AMIS!* While undoubtedly the farming life has many charms to recommend it, there is an ingrained slowness that I find unbearably frustrating. It is true that I am a man who likes the comforts of a well furnished home. I make no apologies for that fact. Giving the little grey cells the fuel they require to function optimally is of the highest importance. Distracting myself by rushing to and fro, it is foolish. But – *but* – when such a voyage is important, I do so loathe for it to take longer than is needed! This is the *problème*.

Last summer, I was unavoidably taken to Weychester, and from there to the tiny village of Finchford Dignity, in order to meet with a young woman who… Well… Her problems do not concern us at this precise moment. She was as pleasant as could be expected, given the circumstances. But the return! *Mon Dieu!* Hastings and I could do no better than a cart. After 30 minutes, I asked the ancient driver how far we had come from Finchford. "Half the distance from here to Morstead," was all I – or Hastings – could understand. Eventually, hope overcame my experience, and a weary six miles past Morstead, I asked him how much further to Weychester. His answer was the same as his previous utterance, word for word – at least the parts we could discern. Eighty minutes later, we finally arrived, the cart having never once varied its horrid pace.

How far is it from Weychester to Finchford Dignity?

ANSWER ON PAGE
204

UPSTANDING

CONSIDER, FOR A MOMENT, THE POSSIBLE TASTES OF ALEC HURLEY, STEPHEN HOWE, Michael Forbes, and Edward Rochead – fine men, all. We are, for the now, concerned more with their opinions regarding assorted British cities than with the indisputably impeccable quality of their moral fibre. Hercule Poirot makes assumptions in this regard, but this is a small and necessary evil. I feel justified in this transgression, given the utter lack of consequences riding on the matter. Never assume in investigation, love, or meals, *mes amis*, but if the matter holds no stakes, it is sometimes permissible to indulge yourself.

So, let us assume that I am correct when I tell you that one of the four men listed is very fond of Derby, while one man loves Inverness, one Leeds, and one Truro. On the other finger, Exeter is loathed by one of the four, as are Salisbury, Durham and York.

How does Raymond Nightingale feel about Andover?

ANSWER ON PAGE
205

THE DUCHESS OF ASHFORD

LAST YEAR, I WAS CALLED UPON BY THE DUCHESS OF ASHFORD TO ASSIST in the recovery of a locket that had been stolen from her rooms during a garden party. The piece held particular sentimental value, which I surmized the thief had not realized. The hope, clearly, was that such a comparatively minor loss would not be noticed or, if noticed, would not be ascribed to ill intent. Alas, the outsider can never know what might be safe to filch, and what might call down the very heavens in wrath at its loss.

I spoke to all the people present in the house for the party, and present here for you a list of statements from those who could possibly have been the thief. That is, I present you summaries of their statements, for it would be impossibly tedious to record every detail of those interminable conversations. Lamentably, only one of the statements was actually honest and true.

Mark informed me that Richmond was the thief. Richmond insisted he was not to blame. Lavinia blamed Mark for the theft. Geraldine maintained that Ward was guilty. Susannah and Ward both told me that Lavinia was responsible.

Everything considered the culprit was immediately obvious. You can see who, *oui*?

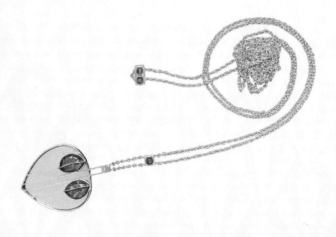

ANSWER ON PAGE
206

MUSICAL CHAIRS

I HAVE SPOKEN ELSEWHERE OF THE PROBLEMS THAT INSPECTOR JAPP has faced during periods of pervasive sickness in the city. Such things can be quite serious, given the importance of police work – even if that work has been entrusted to the good Inspector. So it gives me no pleasure to relate the chaos resulting from that period of disease.

The Saturday before men became too ill to work was particularly troublesome. Inspector Japp had originally been scheduled to work the first shift, but traded with DS Southwell, who had originally been set for the third shift. Similarly, DS Ward switched places with DS Howe, who had been due to work the fourth shift. However, once these arrangements were put in place, DS Ward had to change again, because another department required his presence then, and switched with DS Southwell. Finally, Inspector Japp was ordered by the Lieutenant to swap shifts with the man immediately after him on the roster, since his obvious utter exhaustion necessitated a period of rest, and the man he swapped with to then switch places with the man behind him. So, which officer worked which shift?

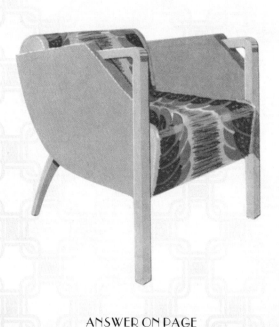

ANSWER ON PAGE
207

ATHLETIC

I HAVE THE GREATEST ADMIRATION FOR ATHLETES. TO DEVOTE ONESELF SO SINGLE-MINDEDLY to the task of working the body in one very specific, abstract manner, that takes surpassing dedication. There are great sacrifices required in dedication, oh yes, with rewards uncertain at the very best. For many, the sacrifice must serve as its own reward – a cold source of comfort. It is a precarious way of making a life.

I recall a footrace I witnessed: a Frenchman competing against a Briton, over a distance of 10 laps of a large oval track. It was an interesting performance, with curious psychological twists and turns. The Briton attacked aggressively, running as swiftly as possible at the start, hoping to demoralize his opponent. His rival was more measured, saving strength for the mid-portion.

For the first 10 minutes, however, the Briton maintained a pace of four minutes per lap, while the Frenchman ran at seven minutes per lap. You will, of course, be able to inform me whether the Briton lapped the Frenchman during that period, and if so, how long after the start of the race?

ANSWER ON PAGE
208

OUTERWEAR

THERE IS A PARTY, OH YES, A MOST MAGNIFICENT REVEL, WITH FREE-FLOWING WINES and brandies, and some serious overindulgence. This happens a lot, of course, all over the world. I, however, am speaking of a mostly hypothetical event that bears a small similarity to an event of my own experience. Anyway, that matters little. What is much more significant is that at the end of the night, there is a lot of confusion over coats and other such garments stowed in a small, dark cloakroom reserved entirely for this purpose. Tired, emotional eyes are not the ideal resource for solving such issues, *n'est-ce pas?*

The 12 guests find themselves quite baffled regarding the identification of their coats, and there is much vacillation, further complicating the issue. However, if 11 of the dozen leave with the correct coat, can you calculate the precise probability that the twelfth has the wrong one?

ANSWER ON PAGE
208

VIPERS

WE HAVE ALREADY PONDERED THE THORNY ISSUE OF MISCREANTS, MY FRIENDS. How is one to untangle those unpleasant situations when a group of people are pointing the finger of dishonesty at each other? The answer, of course, lies in gathering as much certain fact as possible, as it always does.

So, consider the following situation. You are faced with six men, each of whom have a statement about the honesty of one or more of the others. For the sake of clarity, we will assume that these statements are either truth or falsehood, with none of the greyness and prevarication so common in reality.

Francis Holford: Aaron is telling the truth if Edgar is telling the truth.

Aaron Davis: Francis is telling the truth.

Edgar Brown: Aaron is telling the truth if Daniel is telling the truth.

Daniel Brewer: Chance is telling the truth.

Chance Earle: Benjamin is lying.

Benjamin Cash: Aaron is lying.

Which, if any, of the men is definitely telling the truth?

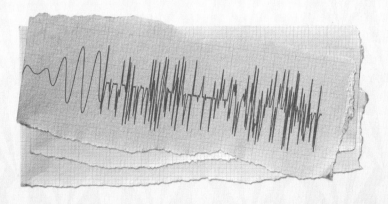

INFERNAL DEVICES

MUCH AS I ADMIRE BICYCLES, AS I HAVE ALREADY EXPLAINED, I AM NOT FOND OF THEM. They are tricksy things, yes, full of discomfort. Difficult to trust, harder still to engage with. Perhaps you think my little peccadilloes humorous in this regard, even a little foolish. Fie, I say. My opinion is considered. The brutal things do not sit well with one who has devoted himself to the perfection of the little grey cells.

Ponder the wheels, for example. If you were to attach devices capable of measuring the distance travelled to the front and rear wheels, over time you would discover that the distances are not the same.

Can you see why this should be?

ANSWER ON PAGE
209

₵OWL

IN THE COUNTRYSIDE, HASTINGS AND I WERE DRAWN BY A
TANGLING CHAIN OF CIRCUMSTANCE – much of it criminal – to a
rather eccentric little farmstead. Evidence previously gathered suggested that
the place was one possible candidate for the source of the matters we were
investigating. What we found was certainly odd, eccentric even, but in the English
countryside, that is not suspicious, or even unusual.

I shall offer you an example. As we walked into the courtyard, we saw a big,
hand-chalked board, which read, "Two hens: one goose. One goose, three hens:
two turkeys. Three turkeys, two geese, one hen: 25 shillings. Whole shillings
only". A quick enquiry made it clear both the farmer meant exactly what he said,
and yes, I could buy a single goose if I wished. How much would it have cost for
me to do so? (I do not, in fact, purchase a goose, to Hastings' evident relief.)

ANSWER ON PAGE
210

SMEAR

IMAGINE, FOR A MOMENT, A LARGE GROUP OF PEOPLE – LET US SAY 615 OF THEM, for lack of a better number. The members of this group can be strictly divided into two groups, those who are scrupulously honest in the discharge of their duties, and those who have allowed themselves to be tempted into corruption. Neither group is empty.

This is the way of humankind, is it not? Temptation is easy and sweet to give in to, while virtue is stern and thankless, alas! But we are here not to debate the merits of morality and its opposite, fortunately. Let us suppose that for each pair of members you assemble, at least one of them is corrupt. You can then calculate for me how many honest persons are within the large group's number, *oui*?

THE LAMP

NOW, LET US TURN BACK TO THE ARTIFICE OF CONTRIVANCE AND UNLIKELIHOOD. Let us put aside the plausibly practical, *mes amis*, and wander together into strangeness. It is in a good purpose, of course – the strengthening and enrichment of your mental faculties through a test of the initiative.

So, you are in a short section of hallway with three switches on the wall, labelled 1, 2, and 3. One of them activates a small table lamp in a room on the other side of a short corridor, shut off at both ends from you by closed doors. All three switches are currently off, as is the lamp. Your task, in this peculiar situation, is to enter the room and identify the switch used to activate the lamp. You can tell nothing about the light level or the operation of the lamp in the room from your hallway, and once you have entered the room, there is no heading back to the hallway until after you have made your assessment.

How do you identify the correct switch?

SENSITIVE TOPICS

WE ARE OFTEN COY ABOUT OUR AGE, I FIND, WE PEOPLE. IT IS ONE OF THE THINGS WE LEARN as adulthood progresses. As a child, we imagine there are children and adults, and we are eager to attain full status. As we age, however, we realize that adults are not one monolithic group. Even young, middle-aged and old do not properly encompass the variety. For most 19-year-olds, anyone over the age of 23 is decrepit and boring; to many 40-year-olds, anyone under 35 is callow and ignorant (let us leave lechery firmly set aside, where it belongs). So we quickly learn that it is vital, if one is to avoid being labelled and dismissed, to be less than opaque on matters of age.

An acquaintance recently asked Captain Hastings about the age of a mutual friend of theirs. Unwilling to provide sensitive personal information, Hastings eventually declared that the friend was twice as old as the enquirer had been, back when that friend was the age that the enquirer now had attained. I will tell you that the friend is 48, so you will tell me the age of the enquiring acquaintance, yes?

ANSWER ON PAGE
212

PROBABLE CAUSALITY

PROBABILITY IS A CURIOUS THING, *MES AMIS*. IT MAKES UNLIKELY PREDICTIONS ABOUT THE WORLD, ones that are invariably born out by careful analysis. In this, it is much like a dear friend of mine whose suggestions regarding the nature of reality and the path that the future is likely to take seem to verge upon the Byzantine – that is, when they are not flatly outlandish. However, time and event almost invariably prove him correct in even the smallest particular, and I have learnt to give considerable weight to his assessments of things. At least, when such matters fall within the cultural and biological. He is not a criminologist by inclination, alas.

This, of course, is also true of probability. It deals in likelihoods and accuracy over a large number of cases, not in the actual answer of a specific matter. As such, it is not a reliable tool for the detective. Of interest, of course. Definitive evidence? No, never!

Consider this. You take three coins, identical, heads on one side and tails on the other. Strange term for the numeric value mark, "tails". Still, that is the English language, a strange beast. You take your coins. Shillings will do fine. They are not tampered with, so when you flip them, they have exactly a 50/50 chance of landing either way up. Now, since there are two sides and three coins, it is absolutely inevitable that at least two of the coins will land showing the same side. The third coin then has that same 50 per cent chance to be either the same side as the other two – in which case all will be the same – or the opposite side. So, the chance of getting three coins all showing the same face is 50 per cent, *oui*?

ANSWER ON PAGE
212

FAIR WARNING

I HAVE SHOWN YOU A FEW SIMPLE CIPHERS USED COMMONLY TO HIDE THE MEANING of messages so far, my friends. I do this not to bedevil you, but to introduce you to the range of possibilities that may be encountered. Complex encipherment is, of course, perfectly feasible, but it generally requires at both ends at least one of substantial time, fine intelligence, and specialized tools. However, most ciphers you will encounter are prepared for (and often by) people with none of these three things available. Thus, they rely on the disinterest and laziness of others.

Here then is another sample to set your little grey cells chewing upon:

```
CIMNK LRQZK ORQIP TZFJZ HPJUR
   EUSYY SKLBP MMSCH ARKFF
   KODWF ESJKV THOZI HUDIK
     TVXDC HSQTD EDKAE
        MJZPP AJBJI
        NDOSL XFAFS
```

What does it say?

SAFE

YOU MUST NOT THINK, *MES AMIS*, THAT THE FIRST PERSON WHO COMES TO MY ATTENTION IS the one who inevitably turns out to be to blame for the crime. All too often, there is a great sufficiency of plausible suspects, each with their own excellent reasons for being circumspect with the truth. To borrow the saying of a fiercely brilliant doctor I know, "all patients lie". Within these pages, however, I have little scope to present a case with its full, complicated glories. *Au contraire*, I must cut to the heart of the matter. I'm confident, you understand, and forgive. The detailed accounts, you can find elsewhere, *oui*?

Alors! I was invited to a robbery scene in an expensive London boutique. The manager, named Bledsoe, was struck from behind in his office, and when he came to, he found himself blindfolded and tied down to his chair. The assailant, whom he never did see, requested cooperation, and gently ran the tip of a blade across his throat. No further motivation was required. At the robber's urgings, he uncovered the safe from its position behind a painting and entered the combination into the rotary lock. When he was finally certain that his assailant had left, he managed to tip the chair over, knocking a strut out of position and loosening his ropes enough to escape.

My dear Hastings was quite concerned for Monsieur Bledsoe, but I was, frankly, suspicious of the story. You can see why, I trust?

ANSWER ON PAGE
213

THE CHANNEL

THE FERRY FROM OSTEND TO RAMSGATE IS NOT WITHOUT ITS PECULIARITIES. Normally the British are excellent at behaving in an orderly manner, but there is something about the Continent, perhaps, that brings out their disorderly side. Chaos often results.

How do I mean? Well, let us suppose that there is a swift boat on that route, one with pre-assigned seating. The 200 passengers each have their place. Sadly, the first person to be seated is a dangerous lunatic, and thus ignores his assignment to take a seat at random. The other passengers are all far too polite to complain, so they will take their seat if possible, but if it is already occupied, they in turn will take a random seat.

What is the chance, do you think, that passenger 200 will get to sit in his assigned seat?

ANSWER ON PAGE
214

SELF-EVIDENT

IT IS AN ODDNESS OF THE BRITISH THAT THEY CONSIDER INTELLECT A MATTER, somehow, of shame, as if it were unseemly to possess native intelligence. Other inborn qualities they are happy to evaluate without scruple, labelling X taller than Y, or A fairer of hair than B. When it comes to the mind, however, they become tiresomely coy, as if it could be pretended that everyone's mental capacity were exactly the same. This is no truer than of artistic potential or singing voice. We are all different, with a unique combination of strengths and weaknesses, and to deny that is to risk turning the life from a dazzling banquet into a bland gruel.

When I think about intellectual abilities of people whom I know to be engaged in detection, the comparatives are plain. My dear Hastings is more nimble of mind than DS Barnes, but less so than me. Barnes is cleverer than Japp, but not as intellectually gifted as DS Southwell. Thus it is true that Japp is not the least intellectually able of the five of us, yes?

BARTON

TURN YOUR OWN MIND NOW TO THE MATTER OF THE CONVENIENTLY AGED MONSIEUR BARTON and his three sons. I do not know for certain that the four of them exist, but neither do I know for certain that they do not, and given the incredible number of people out there in the world, it is possible that they do, albeit most probably by a different name. But Barton is a fine name, *oui*?

So, what makes the family special in this instance is that Monsieur Barton is precisely twice the age of his oldest son, who is in turn twice the age of the middle son, who is himself twice the age of the youngest son. Furthermore, taken together, the sum total of all their ages is exactly 100 years.

You can now tell me exactly how old Monsieur Barton is, *oui*?

ANSWER ON PAGE
215

TRIAD

WE HAVE APPROACHED BEFORE THE CURIOUS HYPOTHETICAL SITUATION WHERE you are talking to a group of people afflicted with the most crippling problems of their mental health. Alas, for such unfortunates, life must be a dreadful trial. Even the simplest of activities – purchasing an orange, say – would be almost impossible for the obligate liar. "Can I help you, sir?" "No." "You are pointing at the oranges. Would you like an orange?" "No." "You're still doing it." "No, I'm not." "Are you mocking me, sir?" "Yes." *Terrible!*

Still, you are in the company of three such men, who are known to each other, but not to you. Let us label them A, B, and C, to preserve their anonymity. Each of them either always lies, or always tells the truth. You do not know which, if any, are truthful.

They each make a statement to you, but you fail to hear what A says. Noticing that, B says to you, "A said that he is a liar," to which C retorts, "B is lying."

Are you able to say whether any of the three are perpetually truthful?

ALES

HOOKLAND IS A COUNTY KNOWN FOR ITS BEERS, AND QUITE RIGHTLY SO. SOME ARE nothing short of magnificent, and nearly justify the effort involved to travel there. Sadly, they do not travel well, and are rarely found outside its borders, although I was fortunate enough one summer to happen upon a cache of good *Lazarus Ale* in Southwark. *Mes amis*, if you will be so kind as to allow me to share with you some information about these fine beers, we shall then explore the consequences.

The drink named *Tor Tonic* is either produced by the Eden Monastery or the Sutherland Beer Company, and is either a smoked ale or a herbal barley wine. The lead product of Adler's Ales is either 9 or 12 pence a pint. *Lazarus* is either a ruby or a golden ale, and is produced by either Hicks Brewery or Adler's Ales. The 11-pence pint is either *Toad-in-the-Bottle* or *Old Clip*, and is produced either by the Sutherland Beer Company or by Adler's Ales. The pint that costs 10 pence is either a golden or a smoked ale. The pint of porter is either 12p or 8p. *Old King* is either a ruby or a smoked ale, is produced by either the Sutherland Beer Company or Midwood Brewery, and is either 9 or 10 pence per pint. *Old Clip* is either a porter or a smoked ale, and is either 10p or 11p a pint.

Armed with this knowledge, I am certain that you can tell me the price of a pint of *Lazarus*, oui?

ANSWER ON PAGE
216

THE FIRE

THE TRAGIC DEATH OF MADAME EVIE HART WAS BROUGHT TO MY ATTENTION BY HER BEREAVED BROTHER, Murray. The lady in question had died trying to save the cat from the fire of her home. Her distraught husband, Cedric, reported that he had done his best to prevent the accident, but he was unable to stop Evie from rushing back into the raging house. She never emerged. Once the fire was vanquished, her remains were discovered in the living room. The cat, it seemed, escaped via the kitchen, and was slightly soot-blackened, but otherwise unharmed.

I asked my dear Hastings to pay a visit to the burned wreck, and have a look around for me. On his return, he was noticeably depressed. He described how the once-proud house had been very badly damaged, sections of outer wall destroyed, the upper floor collapsed in places, the roof mostly caved in. The place of Evie's death was grimly obvious, a person-shaped patch of undamaged carpet in a sea of char. It was easy to understand why poor Cedric wanted nothing more than to raze the place entirely and be done with it. Fortunately the neighbours were a good 100 feet away on either side, for it had prevented the spread of damage.

Once Hastings had finished his report, I penned two swift notes, one to Inspector Japp suggesting he arrest Cedric Hart on suspicion of murder and have his wife's body examined for lung damage, and the other to Murray Fain, expressing my condolences and explaining the situation. I'm sure you can see why.

ANSWER ON PAGE

216

CAROLLING

LET US PRETEND, MES AMIS, THAT WE BELIEVE THE FOLLOWING PECULIAR STATEMENTS to be true and absolute. This mummery is required just for a short while, so please set aside your reservations, and act as if I am talking evident sense.

No con man is ever not well presented.

A person who cannot sing is modest.

No person is well presented unless they laugh loudly.

All persons, except con men, are kind to children.

No mute persons can sing.

A person who laughs loudly is never modest.

So, given the above, tell me, are mute people kind to children?

ANSWER ON PAGE
217

THREE DOORS

LET US TURN, *MES AMIS*, BACK TO THE REALMS OF THE HYPOTHETICAL. IT IS TRUE THAT WE SPEND a lot of time there, but it is a wonder-filled place. Anything you can imagine may reside there, if you so wish it. It has its shortcomings, of course – there is nothing within it to sustain the flesh, after all – but different rabbits belong in different hutches.

This time, we are returning to the place of lethal doors, of unknown rooms holding ravenous tigers or delicious cakes. Three doors face you, each of which opens onto a room holding one or the other, and you must select one to open. Each door holds a notice, of course. The first door bears a sign saying, "This door opens onto death". The second door's sign declares, "This door is safe to open". The third door's sign says, "The second door is deadly to open".

On the wall, a poster informs you – accurately – that either nought or one of the signs on the door is truthful, and the rest are lying to you. Which door do you open?

CHILDREN

THERE IS A CHILD, ONE OF THOSE PRECOCIOUS TYKES WHO LOVES NOTHING MORE than to bedevil adults. But I repeat myself. So, this child – undoubtedly angelic of face and tousled of hair – informs you with a sweet smile that three years earlier he was seven times as old as his sister, then a year later he was four times older than she, then last year merely thrice her age.

Such outbursts are endemic in this sort of situation, I find. This is partly because the young mind is devoted to the acquisition of knowledge, and thus delights in times where such processes are stretched to convolution. However, these outbursts mostly arise, I feel, within practical examples given to test the mental flexibility of the reader. In such a way might a villainous millionaire be said to do something as improbably puckish as to steal a trolley of 40 cakes from a busy kitchen.

Still, this is what we have to face. You can tell me the current age of both children, yes?

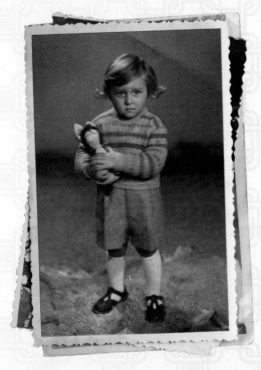

CROSS RAIL

BY THEIR NATURE, THE TRACKS OF TRAINS TEND TOWARD THE STRAIGHT LINE TO AS GREAT an extent as is practical. Train carriages, being inflexible and joined in segments, are not well-adapted to sharp or fast corners, and so it is in the interests of railway designers – who surely must exist, *non*? – to make such turns as shallow as possible. Shallower turns mean faster speeds mean shorter journeys and happier passengers.

So, let us hypothesize a perfect train track linking two cities, which you may label how you wish, but I shall think of as X and Y. It is entirely straight, without any deviation for inconvenient geography or humanity. Two trains depart at the same instant, one from X to Y, the other from Y to X. Their speeds are different, and remain constant throughout. There is in them something of the billiard ball, perhaps.

When the trains pass each other on the track, one train has 30 minutes remaining before its arrival, while the other has still two hours to go. How much faster is the first train than the second?

LUNCHEON

THE SOUTHERN RAILWAY IS A FINE ORGANIZATION THAT GENERALLY MANAGES to provide a satisfactory level of service in managing an extremely complex burden of interlocking logistics. Just dealing with the trains entering and leaving Clapham Junction minute by minute is a Sisyphean task. How much more complex it must be to keep the entire edifice functioning correctly! Truly, the modern world is full of marvels. Sadly, the luncheon provisions that Southern Railway allows are complex in an entirely different manner.

Last week, Hastings and I attempted to refresh ourselves having returned from Salisbury to London by train. At the station café, I noted that the menu seemed unusually eccentric. It declared solely that one coffee, three sandwiches and seven digestives cost 14 pence, and that one coffee, four sandwiches and 10 digestives cost 17 pence. We required two coffees, two sandwiches, and two digestives. You can tell me the price of this, *oui*?

ANSWER ON PAGE
219

INVOICING

LET US ASSUME, MY FRIENDS, THAT I HAVE NOT ENTIRELY LOST MY SENSES. The whimsical is a powerful aid in the preparation of instructive material, is it not? It distracts certain parts of the mind, allowing others to work without let or hindrance, and it lubricates the dry data, making it more palatable. So, with that said, here are some statements that I wish you to treat as absolute truth.

I never put an invoice that I send out into my red file, unless I am anxious about it.

All the invoices I send that are not in gold-coloured envelopes are for trusted clients.

No invoices I send are ever returned unopened to me unless they have been disqualified by the Post Office.

All invoices I send that are in gold-coloured envelopes are for amounts of over £100.

All invoices I send that are not in my red file are marked "due next month".

No invoice of yours that I have sent has ever been disqualified.

I am never anxious about an invoice I send, unless it should happen to be returned unopened to me.

None of the invoices I send that are marked "due next month" are for amounts of over £100.

Are you, my collective friends, considered a trusted client?

ANSWER ON PAGE
219

DECEPTIONS

DECEPTION IS ONE OF THE MOST IMPORTANT TOOLS FOR A FUNCTIONING SOCIETY. Unfiltered honesty may seem like a good thing, but we poor humans have fragile egos. We hide our wounds behind mild deceptions, not least because the truth is often highly complicated, and language is insufficient to pin it down in a precise manner without taking an inordinate amount of time. So, an acquaintance asks how we are, and we reply that we are fine, and both question and answer are lies, of a kind.

The criminal, of course, is far more dependent upon deception, generally malicious. I find it curious that when a person has something to hide, he is more likely to be honest about the things that he is not attempting to obscure, as if such cooperation might make his deception cleaner.

Consider the following. Five suspects we have, for a two-person theft: one statement from each one. Those involved have provided statements that are true; those who are innocent have provided statements that are lies. Person A says that B is innocent. Person B says that A and C are guilty. Person C says that D is guilty. Person D says that C is telling the truth. E says that C is innocent. Thoroughly hypothetical, of course, but who are the guilty parties?

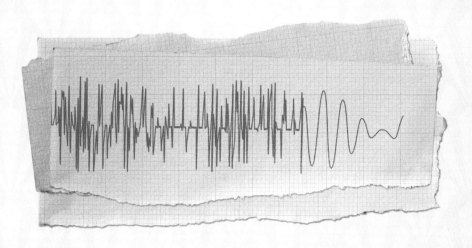

ORRERY

HAVE YOU EVER SEEN A WORKING ORRERY? THEY ARE MAGNIFIQUE, TRULY SPECTACULAR devices, particularly when constructed with an eye for the flamboyant! A count of my acquaintance had one specially designed by a sculptor he'd taken under his wing and then realized by one of London's top mechanics. It was an awe-inspiring device the size of a ballroom, which showed the passage of 45 astronomical bodies rotating around a star, which he had invented out of whole cloth. These planets and moons and even comets were complex and lovely in design, glittering and shining with 100 different colours. Some moved glacially slowly, while others seemed to hurtle. It was a beautiful thing, if rather deafening.

For the moment, let us restrict ourselves to the fourth planet of this orrery, which had been named Lom, and bore a resemblance to Earth in colour scheme. Lom had two moons, whose names I no longer recall, if ever I knew. One of the moons, the colour of basalt, took five minutes of real time to orbit Lom, while the other, a coppery thing with darker poles, took 30 minutes.

Before my acquaintance fired up his device, the two moons were perfectly aligned, so that a straight line could have been drawn from the centre of the outer, through the centre of the inner, to the centre of the planet itself. Perhaps you can tell me how long it would take for the moons to return to being in such a precise conjunction once the orrery was started?

ANSWER ON PAGE
220

THE EXPLORER

I RECALL MY DEAR HASTINGS SHOWING ME A NEWSPAPER ARTICLE OF THE LATEST HERO of the hour, a veteran British explorer who had apparently just returned from a long and horrible trek in the deserts of the Arabian Peninsula. He had been gone for three months, searching tirelessly for traces of the lost Nameless City, the elder cousin of Irem of the Pillars. He returned tired but unbowed, clutching several fragments of clay, which he claimed represented a significant breakthrough in his search.

The newspapers, of course, ate all this up, and were full of pictures of his tanned face on the docks of Kuwait City. These were taken after he had spent a day making himself presentable again, trimming wild hair and removing wild beard, and showed him preparing to take the ship for London. The articles describe the terrible privation he has suffered on his travels. These hardships had worsened early in his second week, when his pack camel bolted in the night, taking most of his equipment with it. He was left with nothing more than his food and water, some clothes, a notebook and pencil, and the tent he was sleeping in. Trying indeed! Hercule Poirot would not do well in such conditions.

I had not the heart to point out to Hastings that the tale seemed unlikely at best. You can see the source of my doubt, I trust?

ANSWER ON PAGE
221

CROWDS

LET US ASSUME, *MES CHER AMIS*, WE ARE BACK IN THE DIM AND MISTY DAYS OF THE IMAGINED PAST, a time of kings and armies and battles. But do be careful to avoid anything resembling historical fact in your assumptions. We wander here closer to the *roman grand* of Chrétien de Troyes than to the learned treatise.

So, there is a king, of course, and he is in need of an army for a battle, also of course. He has a faithful servant – less certain, but still true – who is ordered to raise levies to fight. The servant is given a list of towns in the king's domain, and told to visit them in turn, leaving each with twice the number of men that entered it.

It is a stern task, but supposing the faithful servant is able to manage it, how large would the king's army be after leaving the sixteenth town?

ANSWER ON PAGE
221

HOUND

IT IS A TENDENCY OF DOGS TO CHASE AFTER HARES. THIS IS
USEFUL WHEN HOUND OR MASTER IS HUNGRY, and the hare is a
potential source of food. It is less convenient when one has brought a dog to the
birthday party of a child with a pet of the leporine variety. Discretion is critical,
oui? It is most unseemly to make children cry.

Now, let us postulate a hound in a very large field, who spots a tempting hare
220 feet away. They look at each other warily for a long moment, and then *alors*,
the chase is suddenly on! The hound gallops at 40 feet per second, and while the
hare can bound along at a very impressive 34 feet a second, the speed advantage
belongs to the hound. Stamina will prove critical, and the hound is not at its peak
fitness. As an average, after each 10 seconds, its pace drops one foot per second,
while the hare can maintain its pace for several minutes.

I'm confident that you, my friend, can tell me if the hound catches the hare, and
if so, when, *oui*?

ANSWER ON PAGE
222

THE FARM

DURING ONE OF MY PASTORAL EPISODES, I BECAME VERY WELL ACQUAINTED with several of the people who worked on Old Hookland Farm. If I provide you with certain details regarding these assorted worthies, you will of course be able to tell me what job David held on the farm?

Ian's surname is either Hawk or Bradford, and his favourite food is either cheese or eggs. The worker surnamed Pitney rather than Maddon is either the tractor driver or the hayman. David's favourite food is either bacon or strawberries. The groom is either called Keith or Helen, and surnamed either Bradford or Pitney. The person who is dairyman has either strawberries or cheese as a favourite food. The person whose favourite food is toast is either hayman or stockman. Neill's favourite food is either bacon or cheese, his surname either Bradford or Gibson, and he is either the dairyman or the tractor driver. Helen's favourite food is either toast or cheese, and she is either the groom or the dairyman.

That, *mes amis*, is all you need to know.

ANSWER ON PAGE
223

JUSTIFIED

I FEEL THAT I HAVE PREVIOUSLY OFFERED SUFFICIENT JUSTIFICATION FOR MY INCLUSION of a number of vexatious ciphers in this volume. I do not wish to become repetitive in my urgings of their value. So, permit me to merely present to you a final piece of obscured text. I am confident that you will be able to disentangle it, *oui*?

```
WSSBHT  EOCSNA  S
HTEOOA  WUTOVT  ?
AHOOUL  ITUREI
TEFKGI  TPRCRO
IUATHC  HIEOSN
```

CURTAIN

MES AMIS, WE HAVE BEEN ON QUITE AN ADVENTURE TOGETHER. I HAVE ONE FINAL MORSEL for your little grey cells to chew upon. By now, they should be thoroughly engaged, and you at the peak of your mental performance.

So, consider this last unlikely situation.

You are facing a row of three people, whom we will refer to for the sake of brevity as A, B and C. They are familiar with each other, and are all facing you in return. As you probably suspected, one of them speaks only lies, one of them speaks only truth, and one chooses to answer truthfully or dishonestly as amuses them in the moment.

You are allowed to ask three questions. Each question will be answered by a single person of your choosing, and the answer will be either "Yes" or "No". You may ask the trio one question each, or ask one person three questions, or any other distribution you see fit.

What should you ask of which persons to be certain of which is truthful, which is lying, and which is random?

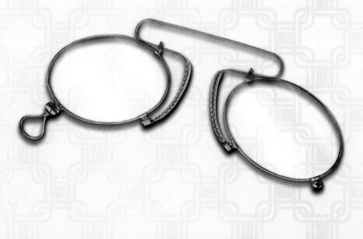

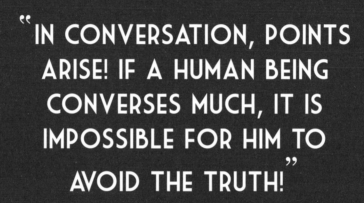

"IN CONVERSATION, POINTS ARISE! IF A HUMAN BEING CONVERSES MUCH, IT IS IMPOSSIBLE FOR HIM TO AVOID THE TRUTH!"

Hercule Poirot

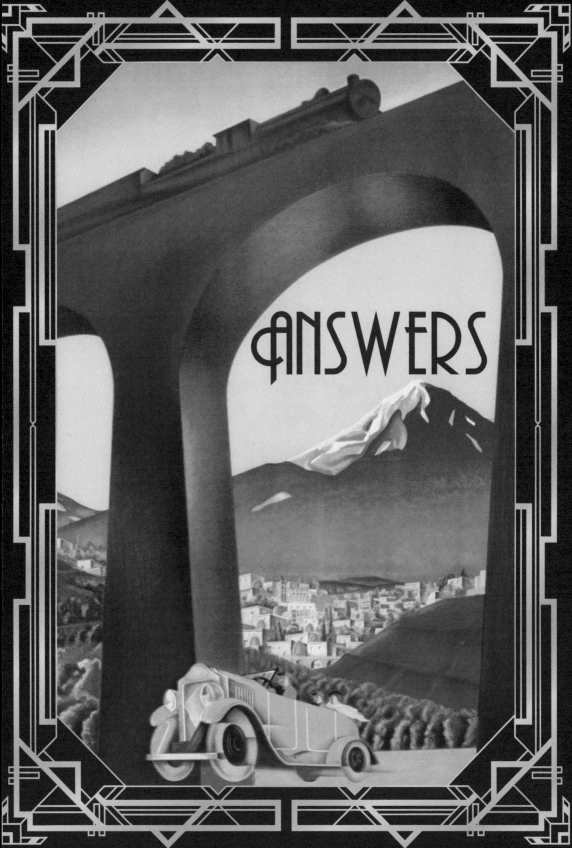

GENTLE INTRODUCTIONS

In such a position, your weight is straight down from your body, behind your knees and feet. That increases the load on your poor knees well past the point where they can help. You are immobile! Ah, until you lean, or bring your feet back, so the weight is closer to the pivot.

CHARITY

A kettle will boil dry, it is true – but the time taken to boil it will vary with the temperature of the water inside. Pack it full of ice, and it will take much longer to dissipate itself. With a little preliminary testing, it would be simple to calculate the required hob heat for it to be whistling for your sister-in-law's expected arrival in an hour.

THREE CHILDREN

In occasion one, the ages are x, y, and z(=x+y). Occasion two, when a + b = 2c, is n years later, but the relationship between a, b and c must have always been true. Since x+y can never be 2*(x+y), c is not the same person as z. Thus x + (x+y) = 2y. From this later equation, we see that 2x = y, and the three ages become x, 2x and 3x. Their total age is therefore 6x, and two-thirds of that is 4x – the time between occasion one and occasion three. So, on occasion three, the ages are (1+4)x, (2+4)x and (3+4)x, or 5, 6 and 7x. Finally, 28 divides by 7, but not by 6 or 5, so x = 4, and the other two children are 24 and 20.

LEASES

Let us say that x is the time remaining, and y the time expired. x+y = 99, and four-fifths x = two-thirds y, or 6x=5y. Thus, 5y/6 + y = 99, or 11y = 594. So, y = 54, and x must be 45, the number of remaining years.

MURDEROUS WORK

The victim was the first person in to work. Everything on the desk is blood-soaked. How then does the secretary know what he was working on, when those papers were beneath a corpse, and ruined besides? There are only two possibilities: he does not, and is lying, which is a very strong suggestion of guilt or at least complicity, or he saw them there when he killed his superior. I said as much to poor Japp, who later informed me that the secretary was the killer, enraged by his wife's affair with the victim.

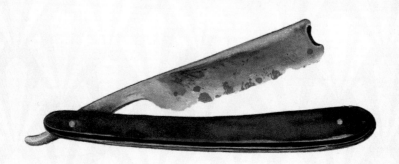

POLICEMEN

We know S=4, Co=15, W=9. Also, J>W, but J+S<15. So
J>9 and <11, and Japp has worked 10 nights.

PRISON

The number dials have 00000–99999, or 100,000 possibilities. Each
letter can have a new set, so there is 26*100,000 = 2.6 million.

FIGHTERS

Each pilot flies a *marque* of plane that begins with the letter ending the
previous man's surname. Therefore Romanoff flies the Gloster Nightjar.

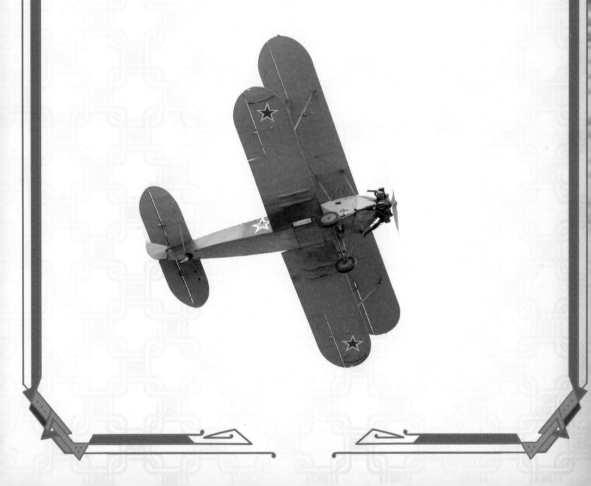

MINER

The left and right side of a river are always calculated as if one were looking downstream. The north bank, in this instance, is the left side. No genuine prospector would ever make such a mistake.

THE MEETING

To find the number of possible arrangements of X items from a pool of Y, divide Y! by both X! and (Y-X)!, where X!, the factorial of X, is equal to 1*2*3*...*X. So, in this case, where X is 7 and Y is 12, the total number of groups is 12!/(7! * 5!), which totals 792. If you exclude yourself, the calculation is 11! / (7! * 4!) , or 330. Your chance of escape is 330/792, 5/12ths or a little under 42 per cent.

INN'S MOUTH

No two sums of shillings are the same, and there are more people than the top sum of shillings, so the people between them would have to make a simple mathematical progression from 0, 1, 2, 3, shillings etc, upward without pause.

Let us think of the person with 1 shilling as person 1, and so on, to person 37, with 37 shillings. No person has 38 shillings. Person 38 could not have 39 shillings, as there are more people than the maximum amount. Person 38 must exist, or else the number of people and the highest number of shillings would be the same. Thus person 38 must have zero shillings. Even zero cannot be duplicated, so there cannot be more than 38 people. Thus, there are 38 people.

TWO TRAINS

Thus, 600ft in five seconds is 120ft/s. Six hundred feet in 15 seconds is
40ft/s. So x + y = 120, and x − y = 40, and so x=40+y. Then 2y=80,
and y=40, leaving x as 80. The faster train is going 80ft/s.

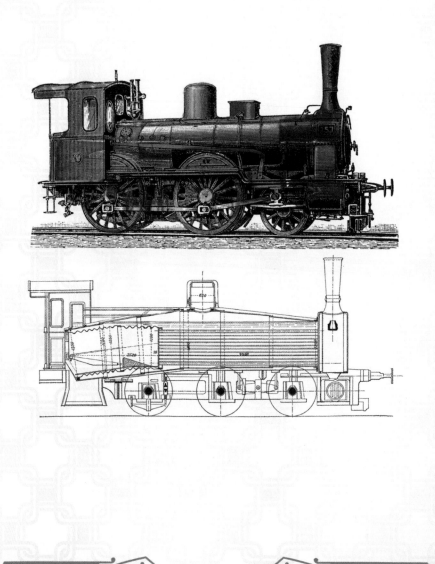

FORGOTTEN PLACES

There is another way out of the pit – through the hole at the top.
If one could dig enough earth to make a pile that provided access
to the hole at the top, that might allow a bid for freedom.

EXERCISE

The ratios of speed mean that three quarters of the time was
spent walking. So 6*0.75 is four and a half hours at 4mph,
or 18 miles, with the total journey being 36 miles.

THE CROWD

We know that $2x + x/2 + x/4 + 1 = 100$, so $8x + 2x + x = 396 = 11x$, and *là*, $x = 36$. Or, to summarize Alcuin himself – for he is the Bishop of whom I speak – twice 36 is 72, and a half of a half of this is 18, which makes 90, plus a half of this is 9, which makes 99. Include the speaker and you have 100.

MATTERS OF LIFE AND DEATH

There must be 15 years between the death of the first and birth of the second man, so the second was born in 1827.

GUARDED

The guards faced toward their master, not away from him.

PLAYING WITH NUMBERS

Call the numbers A to D, as presented. We know C is 4xB, and thus C is divisible by 4. We also know it is the biggest number. From the operations, we can see that A+D = 2x = C, and B+C = 2.5x. So, as A+B+C+D = 4.5x = 45, then x must be 10. Thus A is 8, B is 5, C is 20, and D is 12.

PORTAL

The first note cannot belong to the first door without causing a paradox, so it must belong to the second door, where it can only be non-paradoxical by guaranteeing you your gâteau. The second note thus belongs to the first door. Both notes are false: the first door holds a tiger and the second door holds a cake.

CHILDREN

In the first instance, the chance of a boy is 67 per cent. In the second instance, it lowers to 50 per cent. When the girl's order is unspecified, there are four possibilities – girl then boy, girl then girl, boy then girl, and boy then boy. We know only that the last is impossible, so there are three options, all equally likely, and two of them involve a boy – thus the two-thirds chance. In the second instance, we know for sure that the first child is a girl. Then there are only two possibilities, girl–girl, and girl–boy, so the chance is half. This may seem counter-intuitive, but nonetheless it is how probability works.

A STERNER TEST

Half of them are true. Consider an instance of just two statements. It is clear that the non-paradoxical option is for one to be true, and one to be false. This pattern holds true – in an even number of such statements, half are true and half are false. Any odd number becomes paradoxically impossible to resolve.

THE SUSPICIOUS PACKAGE

A, at 7.5lb (B=5.5lb, C=7lb, D=6.5lb, E=3.5lb). Only C is weighed three times, so total the weights, subtract 2*(a+b) and 2*(d+e), and divide by three to find that C is 7lb. The other weights are easy from there.

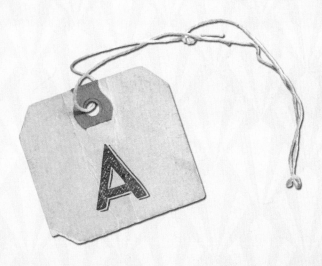

HUSBANDRY

Consider the matter as three equations measuring consumption in entire pastures per day. So A+B=1/45, A+C=1/60, and B+C=1/90. The lowest common denominator of these equations is 1/360th, so we can convert each of the three equations to a form such as 1*A + 1*B + 0*C = 8/360. With three such similar simultaneous equations, we can substitute and solve through simply enough to find that A = 5/360, B = 3/360, and C = 1/360, measuring the amount of the pasture each animal eats each day. Together, they total 9/360ths of a field, and 360/9 is 40, so they'll eat the whole field in 40 days.

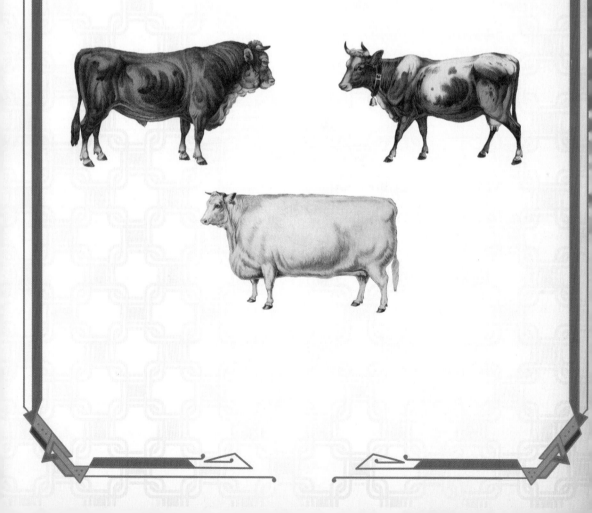

CIPHER

Each letter is replaced with the one that is 16 places ahead of it in the alphabet, where if Z=26, then A is both 1 and 27. The locations are Northwood, Beckenham, Stratford, Plumstead and Addington.

CRATE

If the amount of gold is x, then there is 3 x silver, 9 x brass and 27 x tin. That's a total of 40 x of metals. So, 600/40 = 15, the number of ounces of gold.

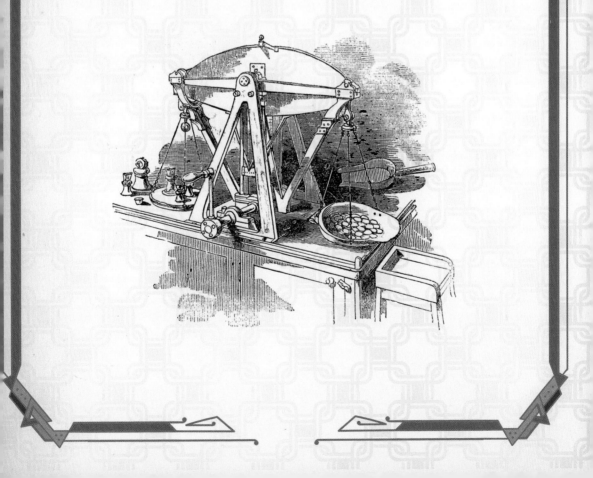

THE WILD MAN

From a lit room, it is very hard to see outside when it is dark, unless there are floodlights. To see the break in the nose on a man lurking in a wood some distance away in the night, when it is raining besides – preposterous! Even my dear Hastings would not swallow such nonsense. The maid had a lover of dark inclinations, and… Well, I'm sure you perceive the general shape of things.

SOCIAL LIVES

Let us label the nine other people as 1 to 9, indicating the number of people each has met before. You may be X, if you wish. Who does not secretly wish to be "X"? Such a mysterious moniker! Now 9 knows everyone else, including 1, but 1 has only met 1 person – which must be 9, so 9 and 1 are partners. Then 8 must know everyone but 1, and 2 must know only 8 and 9, so 8 and 2 are partners. Thus, also 7 and 3, and 6 and 4. This leaves 5, who must be your partner. Now 4 knows only 6, 7, 8 and 9, and so not you. But 6 knows 4, 5, 7, 8 and 9 – they cannot count themselves, after all – and is one person short. That must be you. Likewise, you must also know 7, 8 and 9, and 5, your partner. So, like your partner, you know five people.

WATCHING OUT

I worked 3/5ths of the estimated time, which should have earned the full fee, for did he not see the full benefit? Still, we pretend that is worth 3/5ths of the fee, or £60. In such a case, the watch would have to be worth £50. But it was not.

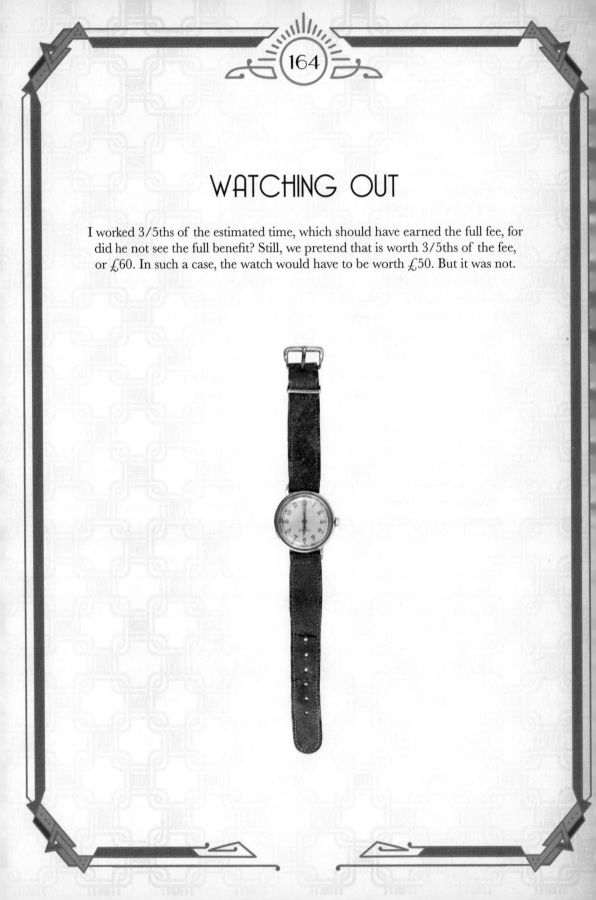

GANG

Jimmy, who had the flat nose, was the locksmith, and had been a farmer.
Derek, who had the bad knee, was the con man, and had been a teacher.
Brian, who had facial scarring, was the driver, and had been a miner. Richard,
who had the knife scar, was the strategic planner, and had been a porter.
Gordon, who had tattooed knuckles, was the thug, and had been a potter.

MAYFAIR

She is now 30 years old. Three years ago, she was 27, and her aunt 72. Only five pairs of ages using the same two digits transposed are 45 years apart – 05/50, 16/61, 27/72, 38/83, and 49/94. Of these, only 7+2=9 sums to a square number.

BRIAN

We have ascertained that $(x+y) + 18 = 2x$, and $x-6-y = y$. So $y = x-18$, and $2y = x-6$. Combining, $2x-36 = x-6$, so $x=30$, and $y = 30-18$. Brian is 30, and Eamon is 12.

INTUITION

The stack is something a little more than 4.5 billion kilometres in height, or 2.8 billion miles – almost 50 times further than it is from the Earth to the Sun.

TRACK

130 miles, that being 80 + 50.

DUBIOUS PROPOSITION

Set aside the fact that such a thing would be cruel, it is still *stupide*. There
is a roughly equal chance of a mother giving birth to a child of either
sex. Imagine all the country's women fell simultaneously pregnant. Half
would have boys, and half girls, and the half that had boys would then
stop. If the others then had a second child, again half would be boys and
half girls – the same ratio, just half of the amount of both. This proceeds,
until the birth rate plummets, ever staying at the normal boy–girl ratio. If,
by chance, some women had a genetic disposition to have only daughters,
the trait would become strongly selected, that is true – but it takes up to 75
generations for even a strong mutation to spread through a population.

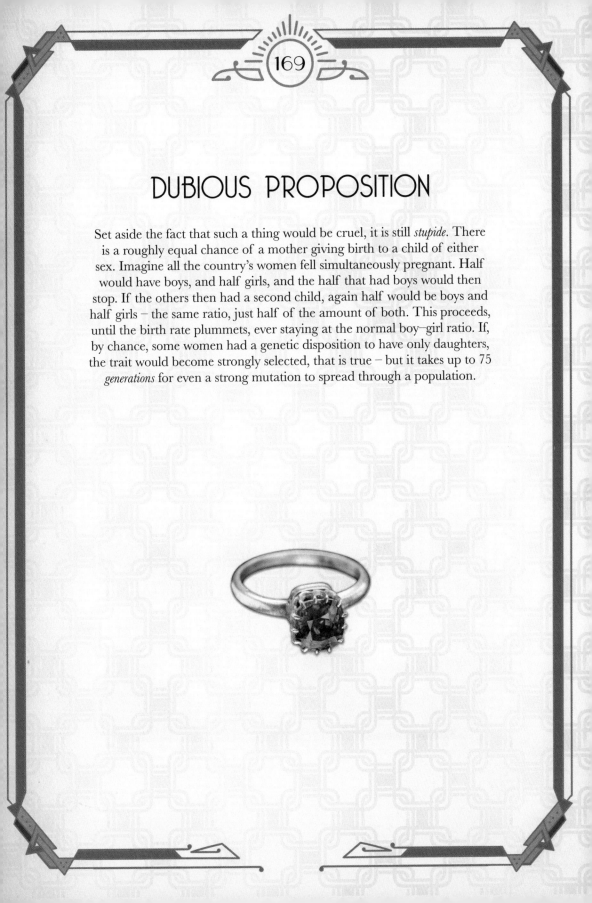

VOYAGE, VOYAGE

If the distance from the place where we slowed down, to our full destination, is x miles, and y is normal full speed in miles per hour, then the time to finish the journey from x would be t = x/y hours, and the usual time of the full journey would be one hour longer. We also know that the actual journey along x took t+2 hours, at 3y/5, so t+2 = 5x/3y. Substitute the first equation into the second, you will see that x/y + 2 = 5x/3y, thus 3x+6y=5x, and x=3y, and t=3. As we would have arrived two-thirds of an hour sooner if the problem had happened 50 miles later, then t + 2 - 2/3 = 50/y (the extra distance at full speed) + 5(x-50)/3y (the remaining distance at slow speed, as x was 50 miles behind). Substitute the second equation into the "t+2" term of the third, and 5x/3y − 2/3 = 50/y + 5x/3y − 250/3y. Simplify this, and you'll see that 2y is 100, and y is 50mph. Finally, from the final equation, we know 3=x/50, and x=150 miles, but we also had an hour at full y at the start, so the full distance is 150+50=200 miles.

SIDEWAYS

It is simple – once one cup is within another. There are many permutations, but place three coins in cup one, and then place two coins and cup one inside cup two, with the remaining five in cup three. Then cup one holds three, cup two holds five, and cup three holds five – and all 10 pennies are used.

THE DISPLAY

Amanda purchased the German orchids for seven shillings. Also note that Katherine purchased Spanish roses for six shillings, Nicolette purchased French tulips for five shillings, Mary purchased Belgian chrysanthemums for four shillings, and Lucinda purchased Dutch lilies for three shillings.

CARSTAIRS

It was raining outside, and his hair was wet. Why would he
and his fiancée lie about his having been outside, in such
grave circumstances, unless he was the culprit?

GLOBAL

You would need to be at the centre of the planet, where all relative
directions simply become "out". The North and South Poles,
however, being actual locations, could still be looked toward.

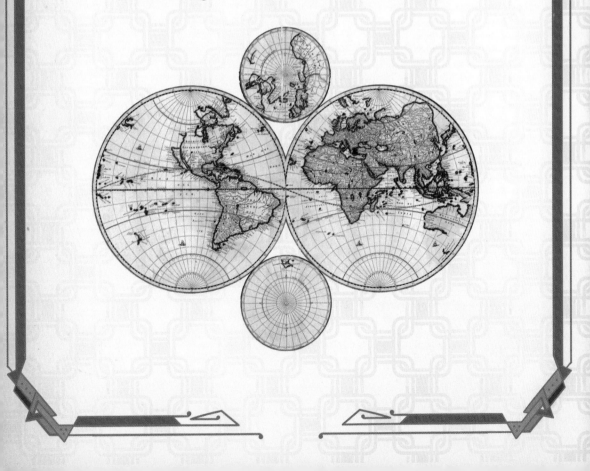

THE BICYCLE

The most effective solution is for the two of you to alternate use of the bicycle so that there is, in total, 27 miles of cycling and 27 miles of walking. For maximum speed, this must be divided according to the ratios of your speeds – 5/4, walking to riding in your case, and riding to walking in the case of your companion. If you bicycle first, you would cycle to the 4/9ths (or 12-mile) mark, and then leave the bicycle for your companion, who is walking. If your companion cycled first, then they would travel to the 5/9ths (15-mile) mark, before dismounting. Either way, when the walker gets to the bicycle, they switch to that. Your speeds will get you to the destination at the same time: 12 miles at 8mph + 15 miles at 5mph = 15 miles at 10mph + 12 miles at 4mph = 1.5h cycling + 3h walking = 4.5 hours.

DEDUCTION

No, my dreams about *crêpes* are unreliable ideas.

THE THIN BLACK LINE

Connect the top and left arms of one of the + signs with your pen
stroke to turn it into a 4. Congratulations, you have altered reality! Now
your equation says 5+545+5=555, which is perfectly obvious.

SOCIETAL

Beeler was the sadist, Leatherwood the cretin, Rathbone the enraged one, and Shropshire the narcissist.

REPLICATION

Quite clearly, it is 90 per cent. The independent assessments
do not add or multiply, they simply agree.

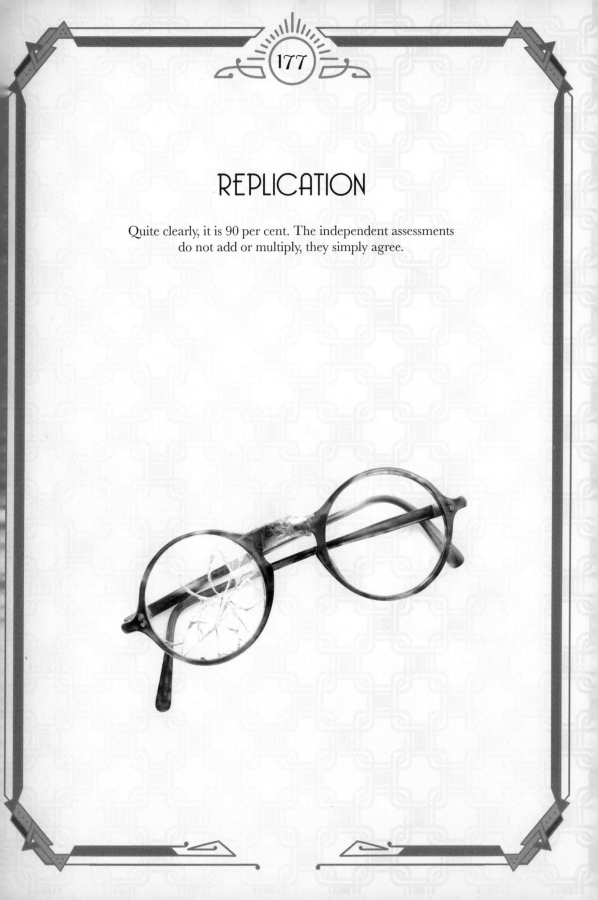

LIARS, LIARS

If X is telling us the truth, then Z must be also. Similarly, if Z is telling the truth, then X must also be. We seek only one truth-teller, which must thus be Y.

FATHER

Lady Cornelia was referring to her mother's father, her
mother being 26 years her father's junior.

THE WHEEL

No. The wheel is spinning at the same speed around the axle throughout its
circumference of course, but the axle is moving forward itself. Compared to
the roadway, the top of the wheel is moving much faster than the bottom of
the wheel. Look at the spokes of a passing bicycle, and you'll see that they are
clearer to the view near the bottom of the wheel, and harder to see at the top.

BLACK HAT

If the person at the back saw two white hats, they would know their own was black. So, there is at least one black hat in the front two. If the person in the middle saw that your hat was white, they would know that they had to be wearing that black hat. So, your hat must definitely be black.

THE MIRACLES OF BIRTH

They are more likely to have three of one and one of the other. Of the 16 possibilities, eight reflect three children of the same gender (50 per cent likely), and just six offer two of each (37.5 per cent likely).

A SIMPLE MATTER

Birds: Tinamou, Hoatzin, Jacamar. *Minerals*: Borax, Nosean, Talc. *Colours*: Cordovan, Grullo, Wenge. *Toxic fruits*: Manchineel, Spindle, Wahoo.

A SECOND DEDUCTION

No. Bicycles are given signals, and thus bells, and
being not quiet makes them undesirable.

ECCENTRICITIES

Corinne Rhodes likes islands, as the initial letter of
"islands" is the fourth letter of her first name.

CAROLINGIANS

Six individuals are sufficient to encompass all the required conditions –
for myself, I would have selected three unafflicted women, who could be
trusted to remain clean-shaven, and three highly unfortunate bearded,
bald, blind, deaf, dumb, and thumbless men, who could at least be
assumed to remain unlikely to interfere too much in kingly business.

THE CART

The sons are the key. Together, they take the boat to the far shore and then one
returns; the son exits to be replaced by the father, who rows across. Then the
other son rows back to collect his brother. The two row across again, and again,
one son returns. This time, he exits in favour of his mother, who rows across.
Finally, the other son brings the boat back to the original side, picks up his
brother, and both row across. They are reunited, across the river and undrowned.

THE COST OF LIVING

So, 6p is a quarter of the money I had at Waterloo, 24p. Add 12p to Croydon
train station for 36p. Another 36p for the bookseller is 72p. Twenty pence
for lunch is 92p. Add 92p for the very lengthy cab ride from Marble Arch
for 184p. Add 6p for the folio – which was as dreadful as I expected, but
a useful gift – we come to 190p, and 2p for the newspaper means I left
with 192, or a half-sovereign, a crown, and a shilling (although, in fact,
I may have had three florins rather than the crown and the shilling).

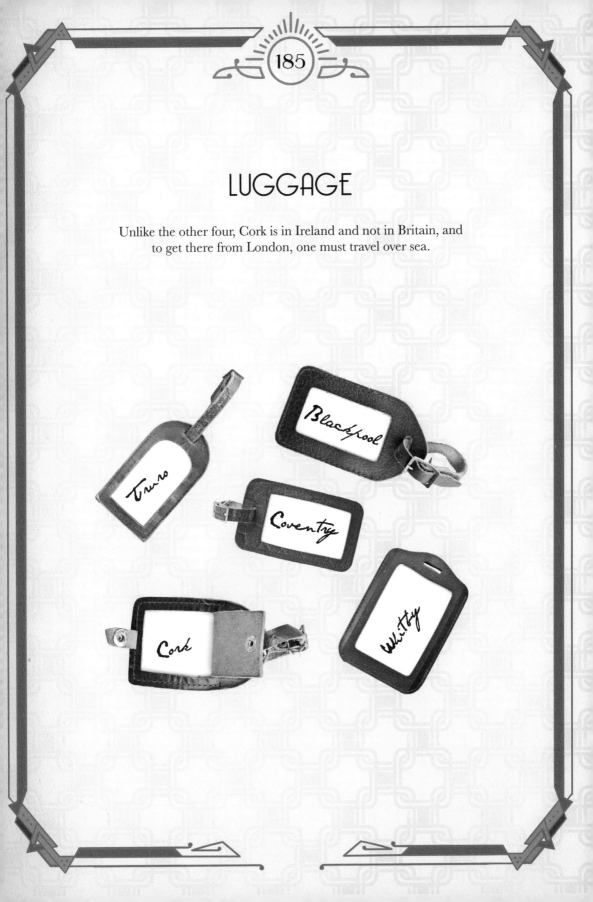

LUGGAGE

Unlike the other four, Cork is in Ireland and not in Britain, and
to get there from London, one must travel over sea.

FRUIT

So, 6 plums + 1 apple = 1 pear, thus 3 apples + (6 plums + 1 apple) = 10 plums, and 4 apples + 6 plums = 10 plums, and apples are worth precisely as much as plums are. From our first equation, replace plums with apples, and 7 apples = 1 pear. It seems clear to me that pears are overvalued in current trading and the clever move is to take a short position on them.

A SIMPLE LITTLE LIST

Forgive Hercule Poirot, I beg of you! There is no valid solution to this question, *mes amis*. Usually, the probability of a random answer being the sole correct option from a list with four possibilities is 25 per cent. But there are two 25 per cent options, so the chance of getting one is 50 per cent. But there is only one 50 per cent, so the chance is 25 per cent. Impossible! The chance must be 0 per cent, except that is also an option, so the chance of selecting it is 25 per cent. Despite the disguise, this question is basically meaningless. It is like asking "Select the even number from: red, blue, yellow, green".

STAFFORD

A postman, on a Sunday? The lie is clumsy and obvious.

THE HOSPITAL

The total number of injuries catalogued is 149. Subtract the two that have to be inflicted to give four injuries, and the remainder must share evenly as three per man. Therefore 147/3 is 49 men.

ESSENTIAL KNOWLEDGE

Liquids, when resting, have the natural shape of a sphere. Water does not have the strength to resist gravity, so it is pulled as close to the earth as possible, taking the shape of whatever depression or vessel contains it, but its essential nature is to form a sphere.

DOGMATIC

I know of 37. You may wish to go back for another look if you have less than that number. If I have missed something, please forgive Hercule Poirot his imperfect mastery of the English tongue. In order of first appearance – for some unavoidably must make a return appearance – the words are: dog, tick, ant, antelope, cur, rat, seal, jackal, bee, char, eel, weaver, beaver, cat, heron, adder, hare, ass, tern, otter, owl, emu, orca, egret, crab, bison, bat, ape, dove, marten, lion, rhea, eland, deer, camel, hen, monkey.

MENTAL JUGGLING

Start with the end, and work toward the front, performing the inverse calculation at each step, and you will swiftly see that $5 - 2 = 3 * 3 = 9 + 7 = 16 * 100 = 1,600$ sqrt $= 40 / 2 = 20 - 2 = 18 * 9 = 162 - 1 = 161 * 4/7 = 92 / 4 = 23$. Simple!

FRENCH GOODS

Monsieur Shaw's office was so dark that Monsieur Taft could trip over his corpse lying on the floor, yet he was still able to look through a crack in the door and see enough disorder to warrant exploration? I think not!

ANOTHER CIPHER

The names are written backwards as a list with all punctuation and spaces removed, and the block broken into groups of five letters. None of the letters are actually changed, though – just backwards. The politicians are Arthur Balfour, Henry Campbell-Bannerman, Herbert Henry Asquith, David Lloyd George, and Andrew Bonar Law.

RITUAL

Two participants are required for each handshake, so the total number of handshakes ever made must be even, and thus so must the number of people who have shaken hands with an even number of people. Removing an even number from another even number leaves an even number, so there must also be evenness in the number of people who have shaken hands with an odd number of people.

BLESSINGS

To get to 99, the boy's current age is doubled, doubled
again, and then tripled. 2*2*3 = 12, so divide 99 by 12 to
get 8 years and 3 months for the boy's current age.

ANCESTRY

Over a million, probably. If we – very conservatively, for the past – estimate a
generation to be 25 years, then you have had 20 generations of direct ancestors
in 500 years. Each ancestor will have had two parents, yourself included, so
the total maximum number for 20 generations is 2^{20} – that is, 1,048,576.

A TRIAL

An odd amount of odd numbers cannot make an even number, so you need to combine two of the digits into a two-digit number to give you an even amount of numbers to sum. For example – and there are various options – 11+3+1+1+1+1 = 18.

FINE ALE

Pick up the signpost, and orient it so that the marker for Holdhurt Row is pointing down the path you have just come from. The other markers should then also be in their correct locations.

THE KILLER

Only one of the four is male. For some, this question will be blindingly obvious, for others, quite annoying. Watch your assumptions, my friends. They will trip you up.

PIGS

Tom gets 1,000, so Will gets 120 per cent of that, or 1,200, while Ed gets 100/125ths – or 4/5ths – of 1,200, which is 960 pigs.

STICKY

You threw the branch directly upwards, you cunning person!

WORKING UP HIGH

The man is outside, cleaning the windows from a mobile platform, and jumps into the building rather than out of it.

CLIFF

Nathan's body was on top of the fallen rope. This would only be possible if the rope fell first, and then Nathan was sent over the edge after it. If events happened as Victor claimed, then there would have been rope piled over the body.

A LEISURELY VOYAGE

It is impossible! You would have to cross the distance instantly, as you have already used all the time available. Walking, no, it is not wise.

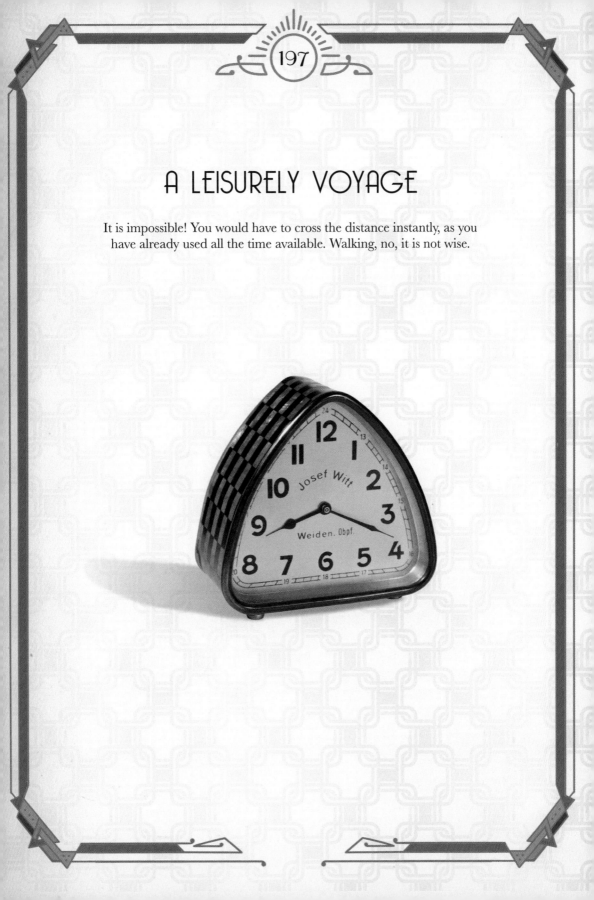

EASTBOURNE

Hastings can outpace the tractor. For each pace he takes, the tractor moves x, where x is less than one foot. When he has taken the 70 paces needed, in the same direction as the tractor, it has moved 70x feet. In that time, Hastings has walked the length of the tree plus the distance the tractor has travelled, so 70 feet = 70x + a, or a = 70 − 70x, where a is the length of the tree. In the other direction, Hastings and the tractor are both working to hurry him along the length of the tree, so his 10 paces means that a = 10 + 10x. This gives us two values for a, a = 10+10x, and a = 70-70x. So, 10 + 10x = 70 − 70x, and 1+x = 7-7x. Thus 8x = 6, and x = 3/4. We know that a = 10+10x, which equals 10+7.5, so the tree trunk is 17½ feet long.

FACTS

They are all types of wall.

TRUTH

There are 3x1, 2x2, 3x3, 1x4, and 1x5. You will see that the number of uses sums up to 10, for there are 10 digits within the statement. The best route to finding the solution is to fill all the spaces with "1", and then count up your actual uses and put the new totals in place: 11111, 61111, 51111, 51112, 42112, 33121, and finally, 32311.

CAT AND MOUSE

The solution is to search the holes 2, 3, and 4 in that order and then repeat the sequence once again. By the end of six searches, the mouse must be caught. If it starts in 2, it is immediately caught. If it starts in 4, then it darts to 3 to be caught, or to 5, and then back to 4, to be caught. If it starts in 1, 3, or 5, and manages to avoid capture for three turns – which is possible – then it will have to be in 2 or 4 for the fourth turn, when the pattern repeats.

DRURY LANE

The man was at a large mirror. If he was just missed by a bullet, why was the mirror not shattered? The story was nonsense, a blatant – and lamentably successful, as it turned out – ploy for public sympathy to help bolster his support.

LUMBERING

Their work rates for the two tasks are in the ratio of 2:3, thus they must spend 3/5ths cutting trunks into logs (for it is the less productive task) and 2/5ths cutting logs into firewood. Three fifths of 100 = 2/5ths of 150 = 60 cubic metres of wood. Not a task to undertake lightly, I suggest.

MONK

There are 184 apples. Ninety-nine must go to the deacons and lectors, leaving 85 for the priests. There are five priests, so they each receive 17 apples. Now, if the deacons are x and the lectors y, then $17-x = x-y$, and $2x-y = 17$, so $2x = y+17$. We also know that $4x+3y = 99$. Thus, $2y+34+3y = 99$, or $5y = 65$. Thus, $y = 13$, and each lector gets 13 apples (and the deacons get 15 each).

COURTYARD

This is a question of triangular distances. The direct distance between any two doors, X and Y, is the square root of the sum of the squares of the horizontal and vertical distance between them. If you imagine the courtyard as a grid, then #9 is at the coordinates 0,9, #25 is at 5,20, #52 is at 20,8, and #73 is at 7,0. So the distances from each door to the other are simple to calculate. #9-#25 = sqrt(5^2+11^2) = 12.1. Similarly, #9-#52 = 20, #9-#73 = 11.4; #25-#52 = 19.2, #25-#73 = 20.1, and #52-#73 = 15.3. All that then remains is for each door, to add the distances to the other three. From #9, it is = 12.1+20+11.4 = 43.5; from #25, 12.1+19.2+20.1 = 51.4; from #52, 20+19.2+15.3 = 54.5, and from #73, 11.4+20.1+15.3 = 46.8. Thus, #9 presents the closest apartment for the four to gather at.

MISCREANTS

The third statement must be true if three is either honest or a liar, for in the first case, three is telling the truth about telling the truth, or in the second, lying about lying. So, either it is true, or three is whimsical. But if three is whimsical, then one and two must be true and false between them. Assume this for a moment. If one is true, then two must also be true, which is impossible. If one is false, then two must also be false. Also impossible. So, three cannot be whimsical, and the third statement is accurate. This means two is the whimsical person, which makes one's statement a lie. So, one is the liar, two is the whimsical person, and three is the one you can trust.

THE COUNTRYSIDE

From my first question to the old man, we know it is 90 minutes from Finchford to Morstead. Six miles past Morstead, we have another 6/2 = 3 miles to go to Weychester, in 80 minutes. Speed is constant, so if 3 miles = 80 minutes, 9 miles is 240 minutes, the total journey lasts 240+90=330 minutes, and 330 minutes at a pace of (80/3) minutes per mile gives us 12 3/8ths of a mile.

UPSTANDING

Each man likes a place that starts with the second letter of his first name, and dislikes a place that begins with the last letter of his surname. Raymond likes Andover. Also, Alec likes Leeds and dislikes York, Stephen likes Truro and dislikes Exeter, Michael likes Inverness and dislikes Salisbury, and Edward likes Derby and dislikes Durham.

THE DUCHESS OF ASHFORD

Just one statement is true, and since Mark and Richmond's statements are the only directly contradictory pair, one of them must be the true one. If Richmond is telling the truth, either Geraldine or Susannah could be guilty, as neither has a false statement accusing them. Since we know that the culprit is specifically identified, it must be Richmond, and Mark's statement the true one.

MUSICAL CHAIRS

At first, the shift order was Japp, Ward, Southwell, Howe. Then it moved to Southwell, Howe, Japp, Ward, and then Ward, Howe, Japp, Southwell. With the Lieutenant's meddling, it became Ward, Howe, Southwell, Japp and then finished up as Ward, Southwell, Howe, Japp.

ATHLETIC

After the Briton has completed his first lap, the Frenchman – who is running at 4/7ths the speed of his rival – is 3/7ths of a lap behind him. After the second of the Briton's laps, 8 minutes in, the Frenchman is 6/7ths of a lap behind. One third of one of the Briton's laps later, the Frenchman will be 7/7ths of a lap behind, and thus be passed. One third of four minutes is 1m and 20s, so the answer is yes, at 9m 20s.

OUTERWEAR

Absolutely none. If all 11 have their own coats, there is no wrong coat left over for the twelfth to seize.

VIPERS

If Benjamin is lying, the other five men are all telling the truth. If Benjamin is telling the truth, then Edgar's statement is also true, since both Aaron and Daniel are lying. So, Edgar is definitely telling the truth either way.

INFERNAL DEVICES

Since the front wheel is used for steering, its course is considerably less straight than that of the back wheel, which is simply drawn on the straightest line. Therefore the front wheel travels further. It is the same principle that suggests the closer you look at a shoreline, the longer its measurement becomes.

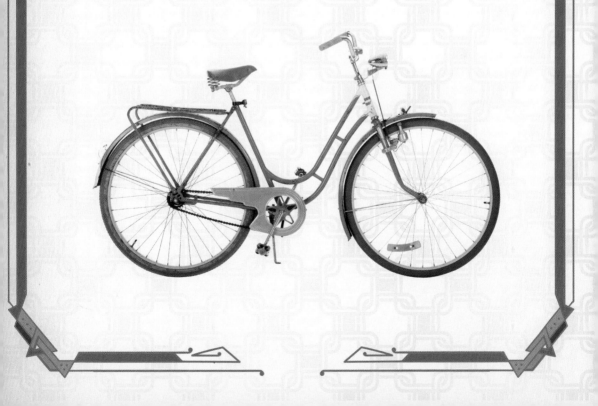

FOWL

We know that 2h = g, 3h+g = 2t, and 3t+2g+h = 25. From the first two, we can see that 5h = 2t, and thus, in the third, that 7.5h+4h+h = 25, or 12.5h = 25. So, a hen is two shillings, and a goose is four shillings.

SMEAR

Just one. That is the only way to make it possible never to pick two honest persons.

THE LAMP

You need to rely on heat to solve the problem. Turn one switch on, and leave it for 15 minutes or so. Then turn it off, throw a different switch, and enter the room. If the light is on, the second switch you used is the correct one. If it is off and the bulb is warm, the first switch you used was correct. If the bulb is cold and dark, then the switch you did not touch is correct.

SENSITIVE TOPICS

Where "E" is the enquirer's current age, and "F" the friend's current age of 48, then X years ago, the enquirer's age then was equal to half of 48. Thus $E-X = F/2 = 24$. From the second part of the statement, we know that $F-X = E$. So, reframing, $E+X = 48$, and $E-X = 24$. From that, it should be clear that E must lie midway between 48 and 24, but to be rigorous about clarity, $E = 48-X$, and $48-X-X = 24$, so $2X = 48-24 = 24$, and $X = 12$. $E-12 = 24$, and the enquirer is 36 years of age.

PROBABLE CAUSALITY

No. Although at least two coins have to show the same face, the fact remains that since there are three coins, each equally likely to hit one of two faces, there are $2*2*2 =$ eight different possible outcomes. Only two of these eight – HHH and TTT – have all three faces the same. Two eighths is 25 per cent, so that is the likelihood of getting all three faces the same. Toss three coins a number of times for yourself, and you will see.

FAIR WARNING

To solve this piece of misdirection, take the first letter of each block, in order. You will see Shakespeare's old warning, "Clothes maketh the man". The last block, beginning with "X", is just there to pad the strings out nicely – a reasonably common habit in cipherment.

CLOTHES MAKETH
THE MAN

SAFE

To be blindfolded and tied down to a chair, yet still able to move a painting and enter a safe combination? Most unlikely!

THE CHANNEL

There are only two seats that actually matter in this whole madness – the lunatic's seat, and the last person's seat. If a displaced passenger picks the lunatic's seat, all is well, and everyone will be in his own place, including the last person. If, on the other hand, the displaced passenger picks the last person's seat, the last person will have to sit elsewhere. Any other choice on the part of a displaced passenger – including the original lunatic – is merely deferring the problem down the line. The chance of randomly picking one from two options is 50 per cent, and that is the answer. If you prefer a mathematical proof, the probability of each passenger randomly picking the lunatic's seat ranges from $(1/200)$ for the lunatic up to $(1/1)$ to the last person, assuming his own seat is not taken, so the overall probability is a sum of the series of $(1/n(n+1))$ where n = 200 to 1, returning a total probability of 0.5.

SELF-EVIDENT

Alas, no! Poor Japp is surpassed by both Barnes and Southwell. From the information given, we can make no comment comparing Southwell to Hastings, but we know for sure that Barnes and then Japp are the least able minds. There is, of course, no doubt as to whose little grey cells are superior.

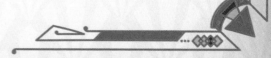

BARTON

The youngest son's age is the smallest unknown, so let that be x, and then the other ages are 2x, 4x, and 8x. Together, that makes for 15x in total, which is 100. So x = 100/15 = 6 years and 8 months. Mr Barton is eight times the age of this, his youngest son, so he is 53 years and four months precisely.

TRIAD

B must be lying, for neither a liar nor a truth-teller is able to describe himself as a liar, and thus C is definitely truthful.

ALES

Lazarus from Hicks Brewery is a golden ale, priced 10p a pint. *Toad-in-the-Bottle* from Adler's Ales is a porter at 12p a pint. *Old King* by Midwood Brewery is a ruby ale at 9p a pint. *Old Clip*, produced by the Sutherland Beer Company, is a smoked ale at 11p a pint. Finally, *Tor Tonic* is made at the Eden Monastery, and is a frankly indifferent herbal barley wine at 8p per pint.

THE FIRE

The carpet where Evie lay is undamaged, yet the fire was supposedly blazing when she was overcome. At the absolute minimum, there should be significant smoke blackening beneath her if that was where she was overcome.

CAROLLING

Yes. Mute people are modest, thus do not laugh loudly, and cannot be con men.

THREE DOORS

The second and third doors' signs are mutually exclusive, so one must be truthful, and one a lie. There is no way to tell which. But that means that the one possible truthful sign has been used, and the sign on door one is lying. So, door one is safe.

CHILDREN

Ratios of age move so swiftly only when those involved are very young. Try starting with the sister at age one three years ago, and it all falls into place – 1 and 7, 2 and 8, 3 and 9, and, now, 4 and 10.

CROSS RAIL

The ratio of the time remaining is the square of the ratio of the speeds involved. If the trains have the same speed, they meet in the middle, and have the same amount of time left. 1:1. If one is three times the speed of the other, 1:3, they meet at the 75/25 per cent mark, with times remaining 1:9. In this instance, time remaining is 1:4, so they meet at the 1:2 mark, 66/33 per cent, and the faster is twice the speed of the other.

LUNCHEON

While there is not information enough to be sure of all the prices individually, our required luncheon can be calculated. Call the coffee x, the sandwich y, and the digestive z. Then x+3y+7z = 14, and x+4y+10z = 17. Subtract the first from the second, and we see that y+3z = 3. Subtract this result from the first equation twice, and we see that x + y + z = 8. Hastings and I wanted 2x+2y+2z, and paid 2*8 = 16 pence.

INVOICING

Yes. Your invoices are all marked "due next month".

DECEPTIONS

If B is telling the truth, then there would have to be three guilty people, not two. So, B is lying, and thus A is telling the truth, and is guilty. If C is telling the truth, both C and D have to be guilty, again bringing us to three perpetrators. Therefore C is lying, as is D, and E is telling the truth. So, A and E are the responsible criminals.

ORRERY

The faster planet will quickly outstrip the slower, so the next conjunction will occur after its first orbit. Taking the initial location as the zero line then, after one orbit (five minutes), the fast planet will be at 0 degrees and the slow at $360/(30/5) = 60$ degrees. After one further minute, the fast planet will be at $360/5 = 72$ degrees, and the slow will be at $60 + (360/30) = 72$ degrees. Conjunctions are thus six minutes apart.

THE EXPLORER

Reducing my doubts to simply the most mechanical, a man who has spent three months with a wild beard in the desert will not be evenly tanned in the face when that hair is removed. If you are in London, watch out for him seeking funds for his next expedition!

CROWDS

As we are starting with one person, and doubling each time, each successive town will put the king's army at a successive power of 2. We are used now to the potential of such doublings, *oui*? So the first town will see us move from 2^0, 1 person, to 2^1, 2 people. Then we will have $2^2 = 4$, 8, 16, etc. So, after 16 towns, we will have 2^{16} people in the army, which is 65,536.

HOUND

Initially, there is 220 feet between the animals, and the hound starts closing the distance at 6 feet per second. So after 10 seconds, they are 160 feet apart. For the next 10 seconds, the hound closes at 5 feet per second, leaving them at 110 feet apart at 20 seconds. Similarly, at 30 seconds, they are 70 feet apart, then 40 feet at 40 seconds, 20 feet at 50 seconds, and 10 feet after a minute. At that point, however, they are running at the same speed, and since the hound has not yet caught the hare, it never will.

THE FARM

David Maddon is the dairyman and prefers strawberries. Keith Pitney is the hayman and prefers toast. Neill Gibson is the tractor driver and prefers bacon. Helen Bradford is the groom and prefers cheese. Ian Hawk is the stockman and prefers eggs.

JUSTIFIED

This is another cipher based around positional obscurity rather than actual letter replacement. From the top left, read down rather than across. It is a quote from Lewis Carroll, and reads "What is the use of a book," thought Alice, "without pictures or conversations?"

CURTAIN

The first step is to identify a person who is definitely not random in their answers. The trick to this lies in their relative locations. So, your first question is to ask A **"Is the liar to the immediate left – as I judge it – of the random person?"** If A is *random*, then B and C are definitely not, whether A answers "Yes" or "No". If A is *truthful* and B is the liar (and thus to the left of C), then A will answer "Yes", while if B is the random person, A will answer "No". On the other hand, if A is the *liar*, then if B is the truthful person, A will incorrectly answer "Yes", and if B is the random person, A will incorrectly answer "No". So, in all three cases for A, if the answer is "Yes", B has to be non-random, and if the answer is "No", C has to be non-random. For the second question, ask something self-evident of the person you know is not random – for instance, "Are there three of you here with me?" or **"Is one of you a liar?"** This will identify whether that person is truthful or a liar. You are down to two unknown identities.

Finally, ask that same person, **"Is A the random person?"** Their answer – negated if you're questioning the liar – will tell you whether or not A is the random person. The final person can then only possess the remaining identity.

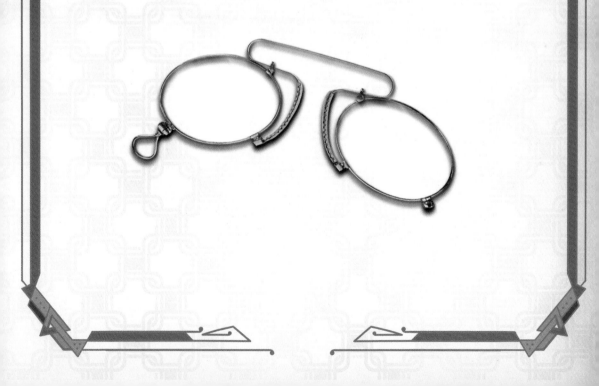